UNISEX SWEATERS
to Knit

Timeless Designs
for sizes 32–52 inches

CLARISSA SCHELLONG

STACKPOLE BOOKS

Essex, Connecticut
Blue Ridge Summit, Pennsylvania

Contents

Preface

*I'm excited that you are holding
my book in your hands!*

Every single piece in this book has the potential to become a very special favorite in its own way. You'll find a variety of neckline options and collar solutions, different constructions, special details, and beautiful yarns worked with a range of needle sizes.

Best of all, you can knit these sweaters not just for yourself! All garments are designed to be unisex. No matter for whom you want to knit—for you, your sweetheart, your dad, brother, grandpa, girlfriend, mom, or maybe for both you and a partner in a matching look—in this book, you will definitely find what you are looking for!

An extended range of sizes covers dimensions from 31.5–52 in (80–130 cm) in chest circumference. All pattern instructions are described in great detail but are easy to understand, and some patterns are even suitable for beginning knitters.

All garments are knitted seamlessly in one piece from top to bottom and shaped with increases, decreases, and short rows. There's no need for laborious sewing, and you can (and should!) easily try on the knitted piece as you go, punctuation to determine the optimal length and enjoy your new treasure while it's still in the making.

Have fun browsing and leafing through. Enjoy choosing your yarn, and have a wonderful, relaxing knitting time! It would make me very happy if this book helped you to create a number of new favorite pieces for you and your loved ones.

Clarissa

Basics

CASTING ON

Long-tail Cast-on

The long-tail cast-on is a true jack-of-all-trades. You can start almost any knitting project with it!

Begin by making a slipknot onto the right needle. The beginning tail should be about 3 times as long as the planned width of the cast-on row.

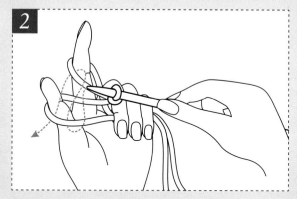

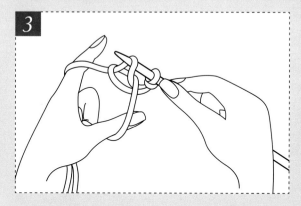

Now, place the working yarn connected to the skein over your left index finger, and the beginning tail around your left thumb. Using your right hand, lead the needle through under the thumb strand, grasp the strand from the index finger strand, and pull it through the resulting loop, allowing the yarn to drop from your thumb.

Tighten the newly created stitch on the needle, and again place the strands around thumb and index finger. Now, repeat Steps 2 and 3 until the required number of stitches has been cast on to the right needle.

Backwards-loop Cast-on

When you need to add stitches to a piece knitted in the round or close a neckline in the center front, you will most often use the backwards-loop cast-on method. While it produces a less sturdy edge than other cast-ons, it's perfectly suitable to bridge short spans and very easy to accomplish.

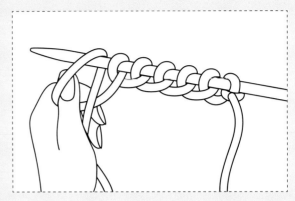

Hold the needle bearing the just-worked stitches in the right hand and use the thumb of the left hand to form a loop. Lead the right needle through the center of the loop and tighten it on the needle. Repeat these steps until the required number of stitches has been cast on. Now, continue to work over the existing stitches on the left needle.

Magic Cast-on

The magic cast-on is used in this book to create double-layered collars. It is needed for the designs Sasha, Lenny, and Alex.

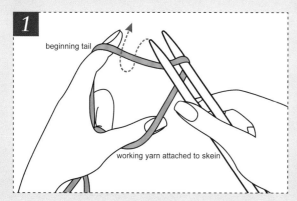

Hold either 2 circular needles with a length of 16 or 24 in (40 or 60 cm) or both tips of a circular needle with a length of 40 or 48 in (100 or 120 cm) in your right hand. Make a loop around the top needle. Lead the short tail around your index finger and the working yarn attached to the skein toward the bottom and place it around the thumb. Here, too, the beginning tail should be about 3 times as long as the planned width of the cast-on row.

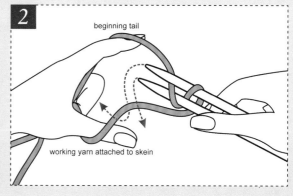

First, lead the index finger strand coming from the top in the direction of the arrow around the bottom needle, and pass it through between the 2 needles. Pull the yarn taut using your index finger, thus creating a second stitch.

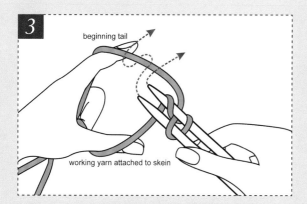

Then, lead the thumb strand coming from the center through between the 2 needles and around the top needle. Pull the yarn taut, thus creating a third stitch.

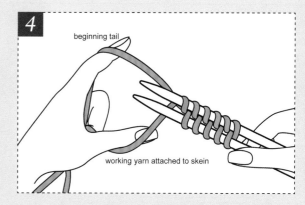

Now, continuously repeat Steps 2 and 3 until the required number of stitches has been cast on to each one of the 2 needles.

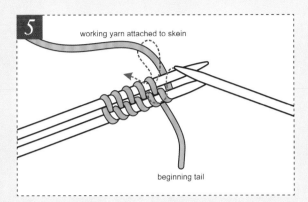

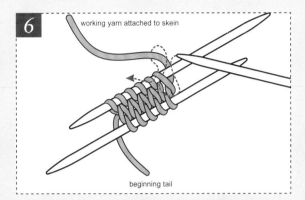

Then, rotate work 180 degrees. The end attached to the skein will now be your working yarn. Begin working the stitches of the needle in the back as stated in the instructions. For designs Lenny and Alex, the collar will now be worked over these stitches until the indicated height has been reached.

Sasha's collar is worked in the round. After having completed Step 5, rotate work 180 degrees and work the stitches on the second needle as stated in the instructions.

WORKING KNIT AND PURL STITCHES

Knit Stitch (k)

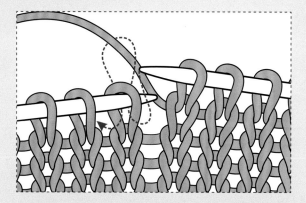

Insert the right needle from front to back into the next stitch on the left needle, grasp the working yarn located in the back, pull it through the stitch to the front of the work, and tighten the new loop thus created on the right needle. At the same time, let the original stitch slide off the left needle.

Purl Stitch (p)

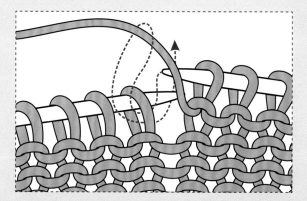

Place the working yarn in front of the left needle. Now, insert the right needle from right to left into the next stitch on the left needle, place the working yarn from top to bottom around the needle, and, using the right needle, pull the working yarn through the stitch from left to right. Tighten the new loop on the right needle. At the same time, let the original stitch slide off the left needle.

SELVEDGE STITCHES

Knotted Selvedge
Knit the first as well as the last stitch of the row.

Chained Selvedge
Slip the first stitch of the row purlwise with yarn in front of the work. Knit the last stitch of the row.

SHORT ROWS

Wrap and Turn

In this method, before every turn, the working yarn is placed around the next stitch (= the turning stitch). The wrap placed around the foot of the stitch this way is later lifted when returning to this spot and knitted or purled together with the stitch.

Wrap and Turn with Knit Stitch

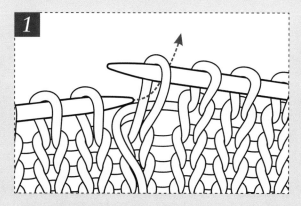

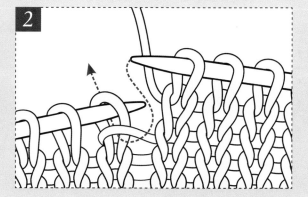

Slip the next stitch on the left needle (= the turning stitch) purlwise with yarn in back, move working yarn to front of work, and place the stitch back onto the left needle. Turn work and work back in the opposite direction as stated in the instructions.

When working a knit stitch above the turning stitch later, insert the right needle from bottom to top into the wrap and further into the wrapped stitch, grasp the working yarn, and pull it through both loops at once.

Wrap and Turn with Purl Stitch

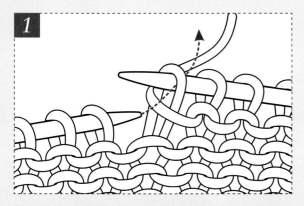

Slip the next stitch on the left needle (= the turning stitch) purlwise with the working yarn in front of the work. Then move the working yarn to the back of the work.

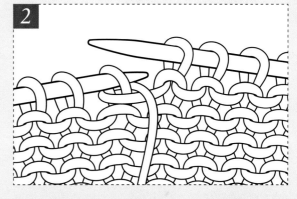

Place the stitch back onto the left needle and move the working yarn to the front of the work again. Turn the work and work back in the opposite direction as stated in the instructions.

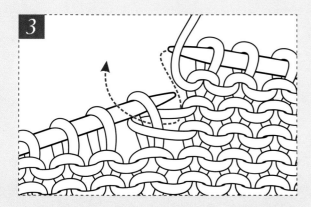

When working a purl stitch above the turning stitch later, lift the back leg of the wrap onto the left needle, and purl it together with the wrapped stitch.

INCREASES

Note: The increases below are used when M1R, M1L, M1R-p, M1L-p are indicated in the pattern. Choose the correct M1 stitch, per the choices that follow.

In Right-side (RS) Rows

Make 1 *knit* stitch right-leaning from the bar between stitches.

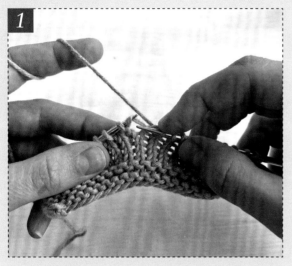

Insert the left needle from back to front under the bar between stitches.

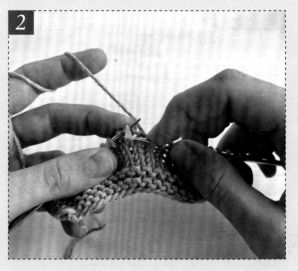

Using the right needle tip, slightly loosen the bar.

Insert the right needle knitwise into the loosened loop and pull the working yarn through.

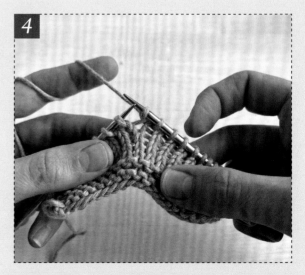

Let the newly formed stitch slide onto the right needle.

Make 1 *knit* stitch left-leaning from the bar between stitches

Insert the left needle from front to back under the bar between stitches.

Insert the right needle into the back leg of the lifted loop.

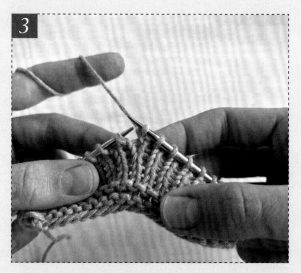

Knit the lifted loop through the back leg (twisted) and let the newly formed stitch slide onto the right needle.

Make 1 *purl* stitch right-leaning from the bar between stitches

Insert the left needle from back to front under the bar between stitches.

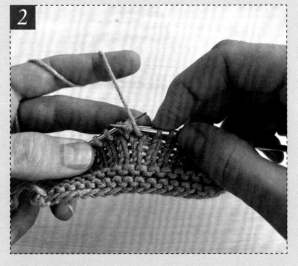

Bring the working yarn to the front of work and insert the right needle purlwise through the front leg of the lifted bar.

Purl the lifted loop and let the newly formed stitch slide onto the right needle.

Make 1 *purl* stitch left-leaning from the bar between stitches

Insert the left needle from front to back under the bar between stitches.

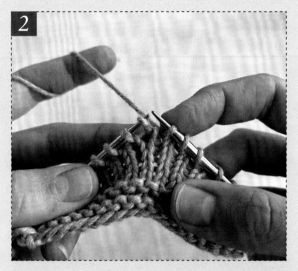

Use your fingers or needle to lift and twist the lifted bar, so that the stitch sits on the needle twisted.

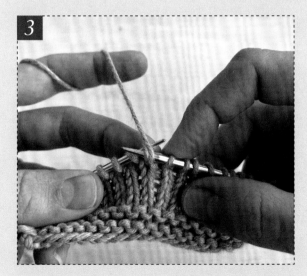

Bring the working yarn to the front of work and insert the right needle purlwise into the lifted bar stitch.

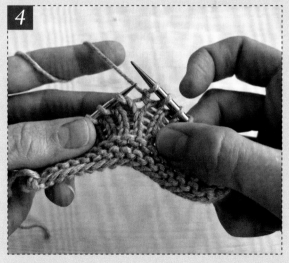

Purl the lifted loop and let the newly formed stitch slide onto the right needle.

In Wrong-side Rows

Make 1 *knit* stitch right-leaning from the bar between stitches
This stitch appears on the right side of the fabric (front of work) as a purl stitch.

Insert the left needle from front to back under the bar between stitches.

Insert the right needle into the back leg of the lifted loop.

Knit the lifted loop through the back leg (twisted) and let the newly formed stitch slide onto the right needle.

Make 1 *knit* stitch left-leaning from the bar between stitches

This stitch appears on the right side of the fabric (front of work) as a purl stitch.

Insert the left needle from back to front under the bar between stitches.

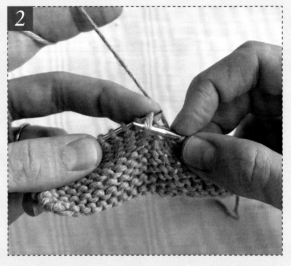

Using the right needle tip, slightly loosen the bar between stitches.

Insert the right needle knitwise into the loosened loop and pull the working yarn through.

Let the newly formed stitch slide onto the right needle.

Make 1 *purl* stitch right-leaning from the bar between stitches

This stitch appears on the right side of the fabric (front of work) as a knit stitch.

Insert the left needle from front to back under the bar between stitches.

Use your fingers or needle to lift and twist the lifted bar, so that the stitch sits on the needle twisted.

Bring the working yarn to the front of work and insert the right needle purlwise into the lifted bar stitch.

Purl the lifted loop and let the newly formed stitch slide onto the right needle.

Make 1 *purl* stitch left-leaning from the bar between stitches

This stitch appears on the right side of the fabric (front of work) as a knit stitch.

Insert the left needle from back to front under the bar between stitches.

Bring the working yarn to the front of work and insert the right needle purlwise into the lifted bar stitch.

Purl the lifted loop and let the newly formed stitch slide onto the right needle.

INCREASES IN BRIOCHE PATTERN

The Karli sweater is worked in Brioche. In Brioche, with every increase, 2 stitches are increased at once to keep in pattern.

Increases are always worked into Brioche knit stitches. Insert the needle knitwise into the stitch and the accompanying yarn over together, grasp the working yarn, and pull it through the stitch, but still keep the old stitch on the left needle.

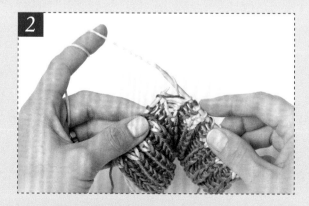

Then make a yarn over …

… and work another knit stitch. Now, let all 3 loops slide off the left needle. In the following wrong-side row, the 3 stitches will be integrated into the pattern flow of the Brioche pattern.

DECREASES

Right-leaning Decrease (k2tog)

For a right-leaning decrease, knit 2 stitches together as if they were 1.

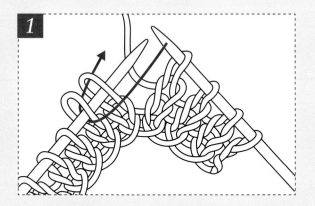

Insert the right needle knitwise from front to back first into the second, then into the first stitch on the left needle.

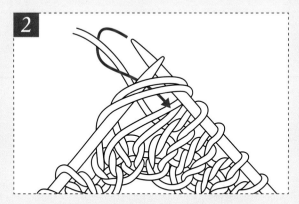

Pull the working yarn through as if to knit ...

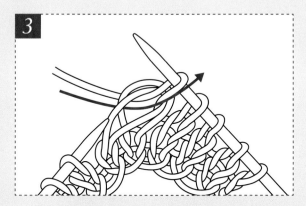

... and pull it through both stitches to the front of work. Then, let both stitches slide off the left needle.

TIP:

The same method also works for 2 purl stitches.

Left-leaning Decrease (skp)

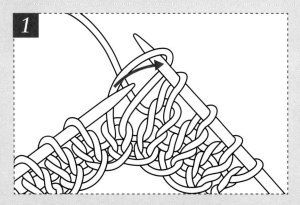

Slip the first stitch knitwise.

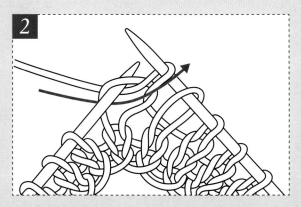

Knit the next stitch.

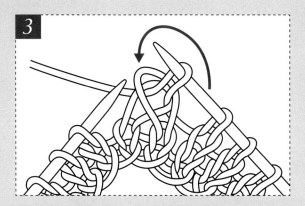

Pass the previously slipped stitch over the knitted one from right to left.

DECREASES IN BRIOCHE PATTERN

The Karli sweater is worked in Brioche. In Brioche pattern, with every decrease, 2 stitches are decreased at once to keep in pattern.

Right-leaning Decrease

For a right-leaning decrease, a total of 3 stitches (= 1 knit stitch, 1 purl stitch, 1 knit stitch) are knitted together with their accompanying yarn overs.

Left-leaning Decrease

Slip the first stitch purlwise together with the accompanying yarn over, knit the following 2 stitches together with the yarn over belonging to the third stitch, then pass the just slipped stitch over together with its accompanying yarn over.

PICKING UP STITCHES

For a collar, button band, or set-in sleeve, stitches need to be picked up from the side edge of a knitted piece. Each pattern will specify at which ratio to pick up—for instance, picking up 8 stitches from every 9, or picking up 4 stitches from every 5. What does this mean?

When "picking up 8 stitches from every 9," 1 stitch each is picked up from 8 consecutive stitches, while the 9th stitch is skipped (not picked up). When "picking up 4 stitches from every 5," using the same concept, 4 stitches are picked up, while the 5th stitch is skipped.

TIP:

When picking up stitches, make sure to count every stitch at the edge—between the knots in the knotted selvedge of an armhole, for instance, there are always 2 stitches, not, as often assumed, only one. Take your time picking up stitches: uncurl the edge of the pick-up edge, then begin to pick up the stitches slowly, step by step, as stated in the pattern.

BINDING OFF STITCHES

Standard Bind-off with Passed-over Stitches

This is the easiest method for binding off. It is always used when no other method is specified and can be used for binding off the rolled edge in Max sweater as well as for binding off the 2 × 2 ribbing in Mika or Quinn.

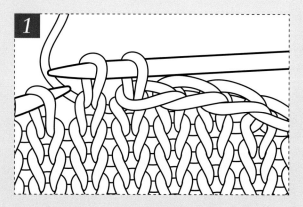

Knit the first 2 stitches on the left needle, resulting in 2 loops on the right needle.

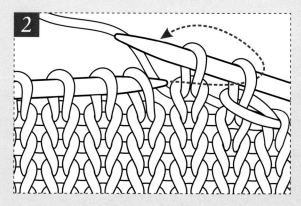

Pass the rightmost stitch on the right needle over the stitch to the left of it.

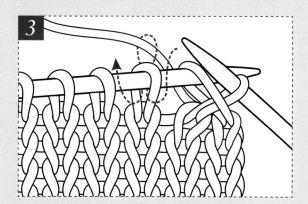

Knit the next stitch on the left needle and pass the rightmost stitch on the right needle over it and off the needle. Repeat until all stitches on the left needle have been bound off. One last loop remains on the right needle. Break the working yarn and pull it through the loop to secure it.

Italian Bind-off

This bind-off is ideally suited for all pieces ending in 1 × 1 ribbing. It produces a nicely rounded bound-off edge that is sturdy but still very stretchy. After having completed the last row or round, break the working yarn, leaving an end about 3 times as long as the planned width of the finished bound-off edge. Thread the tail into a dull tapestry needle.

Lead the working yarn from right to left through the first stitch. If the second stitch is a knit stitch, too, likewise thread the working yarn from right to left through the second stitch. Tighten the working yarn.

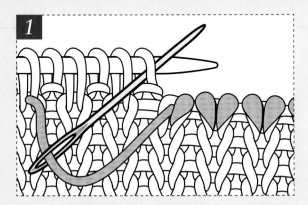

Now, thread the working yarn from left to right through the purl stitch.

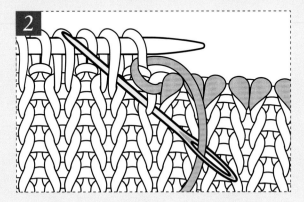

Thread the working yarn once more from right to left through the first purl stitch, then let both just-bound-off stitches slide off the left needle. Repeat steps 1 to 3 until all stitches are bound off.

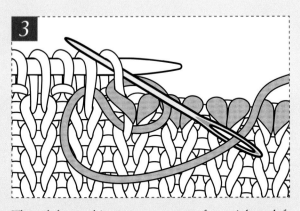

Then thread the working yarn from right to left first through the left leg of the preceding knit stitch (no longer on the needle), then through the second stitch on the needle (likewise a knit stitch).

3-needle Bind-off

To finish the pocket linings of sweaters Sasha and Andy, this technique is used, in which live stitches from 2 needles are bound off together. Divide the stitches in 2 equal parts, place them on 2 needles, right sides facing each other and wrong sides facing out, and hold the needles alongside each other.

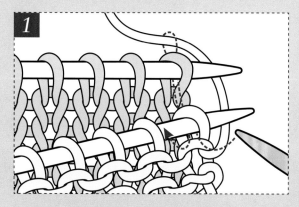

Insert a third needle knitwise into the first stitches on both needles together.

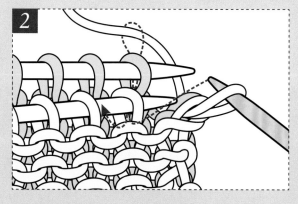

Pull the working yarn through and let both stitches slide off the needles.

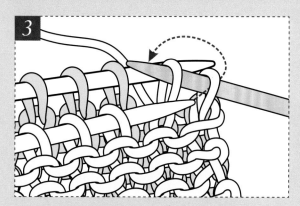

Repeat Steps 1 and 2 with the next pair of stitches, then pull the rightmost stitch on the right needle over the stitch to the left of it (as done for standard bind-off) and continue until only one stitch remains on the right needle. Break the working yarn and pull it through the stitch.

ABBREVIATIONS

BO	bind off
BoR	beginning of the round
Brioche-inc	Brioche increase(s)
CO	cast on
dec	decrease
DPN(s)	double-pointed needle(s)
inc	increase
k	knit
k2tog	knit 2 stitches together
k3tog	knit 3 stitches together
kfb	knit the same stitch through the front and back in RS rows (1 st increased)
m	stitch marker
M1L	make 1 stitch left-leaning (knitwise on RS or purlwise on WS) from the bar between sts (1 st increased)
M1L-p	make 1 stitch left-leaning purlwise from the bar between sts (1 st increased)
M1R	make 1 stitch right-leaning (knitwise on RS or purlwise on WS) from the bar between sts (1 st increased)
M1R-p	make 1 stitch right-leaning purlwise from the bar between sts (1 st increased)
p	purl
p2tog	purl 2 stitches together
pfb	purl the same stitch through the front and back in WS rows (1 st increased)
rep	repeat
rnd(s)	round(s)
RS	right side of the fabric
selv st(s)	selvedge stitch(es)
skip	skip the stitch(es) and work the one after it
skp	slip, knit, pass: slip 1 stitch to the right needle knitwise, knit the next stitch, and pass the slipped stitch over the knitted one (1 st decreased)
sl	slip
sl1-yo	slip 1 stitch purlwise with yarn in front and yarn over (used in Brioche)
SS	selvedge stitch
ssk	slip, slip, knit: slip 2 stitches individually to the right needle knitwise, then knit them together through the back loop (1 st decreased)
ssp	slip, slip, purl: slip 2 stitches individually to the right needle purlwise, then purl them together through the back loop (1 st decreased)
sssk	slip, slip, slip, knit: slip 3 stitches individually to the right needle knitwise, then knit them together through the back loop (2 sts decreased)
st(s)	stitch(es)
tbl	through the back loop
WS	wrong side of the fabric
yo	yarn over

DIFFICULTY LEVELS

●●○ easy

●●○ intermediate

●●● advanced

Before You Begin

FIRST THINGS FIRST

Before you begin knitting, I recommend reading through the whole pattern once so that you know in advance what lies ahead. Mark all numbers relevant to your size—this makes knitting so much easier later!

THE DESCRIPTION

Every pattern starts with a general description—it explains the construction of the garment, it tells you where work starts and where increases and decreases will be worked and stitches need to be picked up. Working from a pattern that you have conceptually understood, I like to think, is much more enjoyable! For garments that are a bit more complicated and contain lots of individual steps or techniques that are new to you, take your time and follow the instructions step by step.

KNITTING CHARTS

When working from a pattern containing a chart, I recommend trying out the charted stitch pattern by making a swatch. To have to undo a small swatch of just 20 stitches is not a big deal and won't set you back much; to unravel multiple pattern repeats over all stitches of a whole sweater, on the other hand, is much more annoying! Knitting a sweater with a somewhat complicated stitch pattern from a chart often requires a lot of concentration. Take your time for each row or round and work through the pattern step by step.

GAUGE SWATCH

We will now touch upon a topic that is often viewed as unpleasant: the gauge. I cannot emphasize enough how important it is to work a gauge swatch, wash and block it, let it dry, and only then measure it. Only if the gauge matches will the measurements of the finished garment turn out as they should. In this book, all gauge swatches refer to a swatch size of 4 × 4 in (10 × 10 cm).

WHAT IF YOUR GAUGE IS DIFFERENT FROM THE ONE LISTED IN THE PATTERN?

If your swatch has more stitches in 4 in (10 cm) than stated in the pattern, it can be concluded that you are knitting more tightly than needed with your yarn/needle combination. To compensate, go up in needle size (i.e., use larger needles than the pattern calls for).

If your swatch has fewer stitches in 4 in (10 cm) than stated in the pattern, it can be concluded that you are knitting more loosely than needed with your yarn/needle combination. To compensate, go down in needle size (i.e., use smaller needles than the pattern calls for).

What if you've noticed a discrepancy of "just" one stitch? Well, if the finished garment chest circumference measurement should be 41.25 in (105 cm) and the gauge is 17 sts in 4 in (10 cm), this difference of "only" one stitch will amount to a good 2.25 in (6 cm) in circumference at the end, which is quite a lot! Spending a little more time beforehand to find the perfect needle size for the project enables you to create a finished item that will be much more enjoyable to wear for many years.

YARN AMOUNT NEEDED

In this book, every pattern contains yardage requirements for all sizes. Whether you are using the original yarn or opt for a substitute, thanks to the yardage requirements listed in the instructions, you can easily find out how many skeins you'll need.

Example: Your size calls for a total yardage of 1,312 yds (1200 m). You want to use a yarn with a yardage of 153 yds (140 m) per skein.

1,312 yds ÷ 153 yd = 8.57 (1,200 m ÷ 140 = 8.57)

You will need 9 skeins total of this yarn.

If you want to knit with 2 or even 3 strands of yarn held together, you will need the stated yardage for each one of the listed yarns. If the yarns to be held together have different yardages per skein, you will need to calculate the number of skeins needed for each yarn separately to find out how much you'll need in all.

Sizes and Fits

HOW TO CHOOSE THE RIGHT SIZE

Almost all patterns in this book have been graded for 7 different sizes; 2 of the oversize designs come in only 5 different sizes. The following table shows you at a glance how to choose the correct size:

Size table for REGULAR FIT/RELAXED FIT/OVERSIZE FIT in 7 sizes

Size	1	2	3	4	5	6	7
Chest circumference	31.5–33.5 in (80–85 cm)	33.5–35.5 in (85–90 cm)	35.5–37.5 in (90–95 cm)	37.5–40 in (95–100 cm)	40–43.25 in (100–110 cm)	43.25–47.25 in (110–120 cm)	47.25–51.25 in (120–130 cm)
Women's size	XS	S	M	L	XL	XXL	3XL
Men's size	XXS	XS	S	M	L	XL	XXL

Size table for LOOSE FIT/OVERSIZE in 5 sizes

Size	1		3		5		7
Chest circumference	31.5–35.5 in (80–90 cm)		35.5–40 in (90–100 cm)		40–47.25 in (100–120 cm)		47.25–53.25 in (120–135 cm)
Women's size	XS/S		M/L		XL/XXL		3XL
Men's size	XXS/XS		S/M		L/XL		XXL

GOOD TO KNOW

The sizes for men and women given in the table are approximate. If you are a woman who normally wears size M, your chest circumference is probably between 35.5 and 37.5 in (90–95 cm) and, in this book, size 3 would be the right one for you. Before you begin knitting, you should measure your chest circumference or the widest part of your body and choose the correct size for you based on this measurement.

ABOUT POSITIVE EASE

All patterns state how much positive ease has already been incorporated in the respective garment. I have decided on three different fits here—at the beginning of each pattern, you will find the relevant information about the fit and the approximate positive ease.

REGULAR FIT:
Positive ease of about 3.25–4.75 in (8–12 cm)

RELAXED FIT:
Positive ease of about 4–7 in (10–18 cm)

LOOSE FIT/OVERSIZE:
Positive ease of about 8–13.75 in (20–35 cm)

If you prefer to wear your clothes closer to the Body, you can, of course, opt to knit your RELAXED FIT garment one size smaller. In the same way, you can work a REGULAR FIT design one size larger to achieve a looser fit.

Patterns

Jona

This timeless and simple basic cardigan works just as well over blouses, tops, and dresses as it does over slim shirts or tanks.

MATERIALS
· Pascuali Alpaca Fino; DK/light worsted weight; 100% baby alpaca; 109 yd (100 m) per 1.75 oz (50 g); in 48 Moss Green: 10/11/12/14/15/17/18 skeins
Total yardage required: 1,039/1,148/1,312/1,476/1,640/1,804.5/1,968.5 yds (950/1,050/1,200/1,350/1,500/1,650/1,800 m)
If you want to make your cardigan shorter or longer, your material requirements will change accordingly.
· Circular knitting needles in size US 6 (4.0 mm), 24 in (60 cm), 32 in (80 cm), and 40/48 in (100/120 cm) long
· Circular knitting needles in size US 4 (3.5 mm), 32 in (80 cm) and 48 in (120 cm) long
· DPN sets in size US 6 (4.0 mm) and US 4 (3.5 mm)
· 4 buttons, 0.8 in (21 mm) diameter
· Tapestry needle for weaving in ends
· Stitch markers

SIZES
1/2/3/4/5/6/7
Incorporated positive ease: 3.25–4.75 in (8–12 cm)
Chest circumference: 36.25/37.75/41/42.5/45/48.75/53 in (92/96/104/108/114/124/135 cm)
Shoulder width: 12.5/13.5/15/15.75/16.5/17.25/18 in (32/34/38/40/42/44/46 cm)
Length: 20.5/21/21.25/21.75/22/22.5/22.75 in (52/53/54/55/56/57/58 cm)
Our model wears size 3 (Women's M / Men's S)

GAUGE
21 sts and 30 rows = 4 × 4 in (10 × 10 cm) in stockinette stitch on US 6 (4.0 mm) needles (after washing and blocking)

STITCH PATTERNS
Stockinette stitch in turned rows
RS Rows: Knit all sts.
WS Rows: Purl all sts.

Selvedge stitches
Knit all selvedge sts in all RS and WS rows.

1 × 1 ribbing for bottom edge, Sleeve cuffs, and Button Band
Alternate knit 1, purl 1.

CONSTRUCTION NOTES
The cardigan is worked seamlessly from the top down in one piece. Work starts at the top of the Back. After having cast on, Shoulder increases are worked first, followed by armhole increases. Then stitches for the Fronts are picked up along the Shoulders, upon which first the upper part of the Right Front, then that of the Left Front are worked to the armhole. Decreases on the Shoulder side and V-neck shaping increases are worked in evenly spaced intervals. Next, Front and Back parts are joined, and the Body is finished in stockinette stitch with 1 × 1 ribbing at the bottom edge. Finally, Sleeve stitches are picked up around the armhole, the Sleeve cap is shaped with short rows, and the Sleeve is worked in stockinette stitch in the round with Sleeve-tapering decreases. The Sleeve cuff is completed with 1 × 1 ribbing, too.

Basic Cardigan with V-neck

REGULAR FIT

LET'S START

Upper Back

Using US 6 (4.0 mm) needles, 24 in (60 cm) long, and a stretchy cast-on method, cast on 36/40/40/44/44/48/52 sts.

Row 1 is a WS row. Place 2 markers as follows: Selv st, p5, place m, purl to last 6 sts, place m, p5, selv st. From here on, increases will be worked in every row (RS and WS rows) immediately adjacent to the markers. Work the following 2 rows a total of 8/8/10/10/11/11/11 times:

RS Row: Selv st, k5, slip m, M1L from the bar between sts, knit to m, M1R from the bar between sts, slip m, k5, selv st.

WS Row: Selv st, p5, slip m, M1L from the bar between sts, purl to m, M1R from the bar between sts, slip m, p5, selv st.

You have now increased 16/16/20/20/22/22/22 sts each per side. There are 68/72/80/84/88/92/96 sts on the needles.

Work 3/3.5/3.5/4/4/3.5/3.5 in (8/9/9/10/10/9/9 cm) in stockinette stitch in turned rows, ending this part with a WS row.

Now armhole increases will be worked in every other row, always in a RS row.

Work the following 2 rows a total of 13/13/13/13/15/18/22 times:

RS Row: Selv st, k5, slip m, M1L from the bar between sts, knit to m, M1R from the bar between sts, slip m, k5, selv st.

WS Row: Work all sts as they appear (knitting the knits and purling the purls), slipping all markers when you encounter them.

You now have 94/98/106/110/118/128/140 sts on the needles. Break the working yarn and transfer these stitches to a piece of waste yarn, an extra needle, or a spare cord for holding.

Upper Right Front

For this part, pick up and knit 18/18/22/22/24/24/24 sts from the slanted part of the Back Right Shoulder. Begin picking up at the Shoulder point of the armhole and continuously pick up 1 st each from every selvedge stitch of the Back. Finish picking up at the neckline opening.

Row 1 is a WS row. Place 2 markers as follows: Selv st, p5, place m, purl to last 5 sts, place m, p4, selv st. From here on, decreases will be worked at the right

edge of the Right Front in every 6th row (always in a RS row), 4 times in all. Begin by working **Rows 2–5**, all sts as they appear (knitting the knits and purling the purls). Slip all markers when you encounter them.

Row 6 (RS): Knit to m, slip m, ssk, knit to end of row.

Rows 7–11: Work all sts as they appear.

Rows 12 (RS): Work as Row 6.

Rows 13–17: Work all sts as they appear.

Row 18 (RS): Work as Row 6.

Rows 19–23: Work all sts as they appear.

Row 24 (RS): Work as Row 6.

Rows 25–27: Work all sts as they appear.

All decreases have now been completed. There are 14/14/18/18/20/20/20 sts on the needles.

From here on, begin V-neck shaping increases, increasing in every 4th row, 15/17/18/19/19/21/23 times in all. Work V-neck shaping increases at the neck side as follows: **Inc row (RS):** Selv st, knit to 2nd marker, M1R from the bar between sts, slip m, k5, selv st.

Rows 28, 32, 36, 40, 44, 48, 52, 56 (RS): Selv st, knit to 2nd marker, M1R from the bar between sts, slip m, k5, selv st.

Rows 29–31, 33–35, 37–39, 41–43, 45–47, 49–51, 53–55, 57–59: Work all sts as they appear (knitting the knits and purling the purls).

You have now completed 8 increases at the neck side. There are 22/22/26/26/28/28/28 sts on the needles.

In the following section, finishing the Fronts as described for each size separately:

Size 1:
From here on, in addition to the neckline increases, armhole increases will be worked concurrently. Armhole increases are to be worked in every other row (always in a RS row) a total of 13 times. At the same time, the last 7 neckline increases will be worked as before in every 4th row. In the following instructions, only RS are written out. In all WS rows, work all sts as they appear (knitting the knits and purling the purls).

Row 60 (RS): Selv st, k4, remove m, k1, place m, M1L from the bar between sts, knit to m, M1R from the bar between sts, slip m, k5, selv st.

Row 62 (RS): Selv st, k5, slip m, M1L from the bar between sts, knit to end of row.

Row 64 (RS): Selv st, k5, slip m, M1L from the bar between sts, knit to m, M1R from the bar between sts, slip m, k5, selv st.

Rows 66, 70, 74, 78, 82 (RS): Work as Row 62.

Rows 68, 72, 76, 80, 84 (RS): Work as Row 64.

Size 2:
Armhole increases are to be worked in every other row (always in a RS row) a total of 13 times. At the same time, the last 9 neckline increases will be worked as before in every 4th row. Only RS are written out. In all WS rows, work all sts as they appear (knitting the knits and purling the purls).

Rows 60, 64 (RS): Selv st, knit to 2nd marker, M1R from the bar between sts, slip m, k5, selv st.

Rows 61–63, 65–67: Work all sts as they appear (knitting the knits and purling the purls).

Row 68 (RS): Selv st, k4, remove m, k1, place m, M1L from the bar between sts, knit to m, M1R from the bar between sts, slip m, k5, selv st.

Row 70 (RS): Selv st, k5, slip m, M1L from the bar between sts, knit to end of row.

Row 72 (RS): Selv st, k5, slip m, M1L from the bar between sts, knit to m, M1R from the bar between sts, slip m, k5, selv st.

Rows 74, 78, 82, 86, 90 (RS): Work as Row 70.

Rows 76, 80, 84, 88, 92 (RS): Work as Row 72.

Size 3:
Armhole increases are to be worked in every other row (always in a RS row) a total of 13 times. At the same time, the last 10 neckline increases will be worked as before in every 4th row. Only RS are written out. In all WS rows, work all sts as they appear (knitting the knits and purling the purls).

Rows 60, 64, 68 (RS): Selv st, knit to 2nd marker, M1R from the bar between sts, slip m, k5, selv st.

Rows 61–63, 65–67, 69–71: Work all sts as they appear (knitting the knits and purling the purls).

Row 72 (RS): Selv st, k4, remove m, k1, place m, M1L from the bar between sts, knit to m, M1R from the bar between sts, slip m, k5, selv st.

Row 74 (RS): Selv st, k5, slip m, M1L from the bar between sts, knit to end of row.

Row 76 (RS): Selv st, k5, slip m, M1L from the bar between sts, knit to m, M1R from the bar between sts, slip m, k5, selv st.

Rows 78, 82, 86, 90, 94 (RS): Work as Row 74.

Rows 80, 84, 88, 92, 96 (RS): Work as Row 76.

Size 4:
Armhole increases are to be worked in every other row (always in a RS row) a total of 13 times. At the same time, the last 11 neckline increases will be worked as before in every 4th row. Only RS are written out. In all WS rows, work all sts as they appear (knitting the knits and purling the purls).

Rows 60, 64, 68, 72 (RS): Selv st, knit to 2nd marker, M1R from the bar between sts, slip m, k5, selv st.

Rows 61–63, 65–67, 69–71, 73–75: Work all sts as they appear (knitting the knits and purling the purls).

Row 76 (RS): Selv st, k4, remove m, k1, place m, M1L from the bar between sts, knit to m, M1R from the bar between sts, slip m, k5, selv st.

Row 78 (RS): Selv st, k5, slip m, M1L from the bar between sts, knit to end of row.

Row 80 (RS): Selv st, k5, slip m, M1L from the bar between sts, knit to m, M1R from the bar between sts, slip m, k5, selv st.

Rows 82, 86, 90, 94, 98 (RS): Work as Row 78.

Rows 84, 88, 92, 96, 100 (RS): Work as Row 80.

Size 5:

Armhole increases are to be worked in every other row (always in a RS row) a total of 15 times. At the same time, the last 11 neckline increases will be worked as before in every 4th row. Only RS are written out. In all WS rows, work all sts as they appear (knitting the knits and purling the purls).

Rows 60, 64, 68, 72, 76 (RS): Selv st, knit to 2nd marker, M1R from the bar between sts, slip m, k5, selv st.

Rows 61–63, 65–67, 69–71, 73–75, 77–79: Work all sts as they appear (knitting the knits and purling the purls).

Row 80 (RS): Selv st, k4, remove m, k1, place m, M1L from the bar between sts, knit to m, M1R from the bar between sts, slip m, k5, selv st.

Row 82 (RS): Selv st, k5, slip m, M1L from the bar between sts, knit to end of row.

Row 84 (RS): Selv st, k5, slip m, M1L from the bar between sts, knit to m, M1R from the bar between sts, slip m, k5, selv st.

Rows 86, 90, 94, 98, 102, 104, 106, 108 (RS): Work as Row 82.

Rows 88, 92, 96, 10 (RS): Work as Row 84.

Size 6:

Armhole increases are to be worked in every other row (always in a RS row) a total of 18 times. At the same time, the last 13 neckline increases will be worked as before in every 4th row. In the following instructions, only RS are written out. In all WS rows, work all sts as they appear (knitting the knits and purling the purls).

Rows 60, 64, 68, 72 (RS): Selv st, knit to 2nd marker, M1R from the bar between sts, slip m, k5, selv st.

Rows 61–63, 65–67, 69–71, 73–75: Work all sts as they appear (knitting the knits and purling the purls).

Row 76 (RS): Selv st, k4, remove m, k1, place m, M1L from the bar between sts, knit to m, M1R from the bar between sts, slip m, k5, selv st.

Row 78 (RS): Selv st, k5, slip m, M1L from the bar between sts, knit to end of row.

Row 80 (RS): Selv st, k5, slip m, M1L from the bar between sts, knit to m, M1R from the bar between sts, slip m, k5, selv st.

Rows 82, 86, 90, 94, 98, 102, 106, 110 (RS): Work as Row 78.

Rows 84, 88, 92, 96, 100, 104, 108 (RS): Work as Row 80.

Size 7:

Armhole increases are to be worked in every other row (always in a RS row) a total of 22 times. At the same time, the last 15 neckline increases will be worked as before in every 4th row. Only RS are written out. In all WS rows, work all sts as they appear (knitting the knits and purling the purls).

Rows 60, 64, 68, 72 (RS): Selv st, knit to 2nd marker, M1R from the bar between sts, slip m, k5, selv st.

Rows 61–63, 65–67, 69–71, 73–75: Work all sts as they appear (knitting the knits and purling the purls).

Row 76 (RS): Selv st, k4, remove m, k1, place m, M1L from the bar between sts, knit to m, M1R from the bar between sts, slip m, k5, selv st.

Row 78 (RS): Selv st, k5, slip m, M1L from the bar between sts, knit to end of row.

Row 80 (RS): Selv st, k5, slip m, M1L from the bar between sts, knit to m, M1R from the bar between sts, slip m, k5, selv st.

Rows 82, 86, 90, 94, 98, 102, 106, 110, 114, 118 (RS): Work as Row 78.

Rows 84, 88, 92, 96, 100, 104, 108, 112, 116 (RS): Work as Row 80.

Continue for all sizes:

All increases for V-neck and armhole have now been completed. You now have a total of 42/44/49/50/54/59/65 sts on the needles. Break the working yarn and transfer these stitches to a piece of waste yarn, an extra needle, or a spare cord for holding.

Upper Left Front

For this part, pick up and knit 18/18/22/22/24/24/24 sts from the slanted section of the Shoulder on the left half of the Back. Begin picking up at the neckline opening and continuously pick up 1 st each from every selvedge stitch of the Back. Finish picking up at the Shoulder point of the armhole.

Row 1 is a WS row. Place 2 markers as follows: Selv st, p4, place m, purl to last 6 sts, place m, p5, selv st.

From here on, decreases will be worked at the left edge of the Left Front in every 6th row (always in a RS row), 4 times in all.

Begin by working **Rows 2–5**, all sts as they appear (knitting the knits and purling the purls). Slip all markers when you encounter them.

Row 6 (RS): Knit to 2 sts before the 2nd marker, k2tog, slip m, k4, selv st.

Rows 7–11: Work all sts as they appear.

Row 12 (RS): Work as Row 6.

Rows 13–17: Work all sts as they appear.

Row 18 (RS): Work as Row 6.

Rows 19–23: Work all sts as they appear.

Row 24 (RS): Work as Row 6.

Rows 25–27: Work all sts as they appear.

All decreases have now been completed. There are 14/14/18/18/20/20/20 sts on the needles.

From here on, begin V-neck shaping increases, increasing in every 4th row, 15/17/18/19/19/21/23 times in all.

Work V-neck shaping increases at the neck side as follows: **Inc row (RS):** Selv st, k5, slip m, M1L from the bar between sts, knit to end of row.

Rows 28, 32, 36, 40, 44, 48, 52, 56 (RS): Selv st, k5, slip m, M1L from the bar between sts, knit to end of row.

Rows 29–31, 33–35, 37–39, 41–43, 45–47, 49–51, 53–55, 57–59: Work all sts as they appear.

You have now completed 8 increases at the neck side. There are 22/22/26/26/28/28/28 sts on the needles.

In the following section, finishing the Fronts is decribed for each size separately:

Size 1:

From here on, in addition to the neckline increases, armhole increases will be worked at the same time. Armhole increases are to be worked in every other row (always in a RS row) a total of 13 times. At the same time, the last 7 neckline increases will be worked as before in every 4th row. Only RS are written out. In all WS rows, work all sts as they appear (knitting the knits and purling the purls).

Row 60 (RS): Selv st, k5, slip m, M1L from the bar between sts, knit to 1 st before next m, M1R from the bar between sts, place m, k1, remove m, k4, selv st.

Row 62 (RS): Selv st, k5, slip m, M1L from the bar between sts, knit to end of row.

Row 64 (RS): Selv st, k5, slip m, M1L from the bar between sts, knit to m, M1R from the bar between sts, slip m, k5, selv st.

Rows 66, 70, 74, 78, 82 (RS): Work as Row 62.

Rows 68, 72, 76, 80, 84 (RS): Work as Row 64.

Size 2:

Armhole increases are to be worked in every other row (always in a RS row) a total of 13 times. At the same time, the last 9 neckline increases will be worked as before in every 4th row. Only RS rows are written out. In all WS rows, work all sts as they appear (knitting the knits and purling the purls).

Rows 60, 64 (RS): Selv st, knit to 2nd marker, M1R from the bar between sts, slip m, k5, selv st.

Rows 61–63, 65–67: Work all sts as they appear (knitting the knits and purling the purls).

Row 68 (RS): Selv st, k5, slip m, M1L from the bar between sts, knit to 1 st before next m, M1R from the bar between sts, place m, k1, remove m, k4, selv st.

Row 70 (RS): Selv st, k5, slip m, M1L from the bar between sts, knit to end of row.

Row 72 (RS): Selv st, k5, slip m, M1L from the bar between sts, knit to m, M1R from the bar between sts, slip m, k5, selv st.

Rows 74, 78, 82, 86, 90 (RS): Work as Row 70.

Rows 76, 80, 84, 88, 92 (RS): Work as Row 72.

Size 3:

Armhole increases are to be worked in every other row (always in a RS row) a total of 13 times. At the same time, the last 10 neckline increases will be worked as before in every 4th row. Only RS rows are written out. In all WS rows, work all sts as they appear (knitting the knits and purling the purls).

Rows 60, 64, 68 (RS): Selv st, knit to 2nd marker, M1R from the bar between sts, slip m, k5, selv st.

Rows 61–63, 65–67, 69–71: Work all sts as they appear (knitting the knits and purling the purls).

Row 72 (RS): Selv st, k5, slip m, M1L from the bar between sts, knit to 1 st before next m, M1R from the bar between sts, place m, k1, remove m, k4, selv st.

Row 74 (RS): Selv st, k5, slip m, M1L from the bar between sts, knit to end of row.

Row 76 (RS): Selv st, k5, slip m, M1L from the bar between sts, knit to m, M1R from the bar between sts, slip m, k5, selv st.

Rows 78, 82, 86, 90, 94 (RS): Work as Row 74.

Rows 80, 84, 88, 92, 96 (RS): Work as Row 76.

Size 4:

Armhole increases are to be worked in every other row (always in a RS row) a total of 13 times. At the same time, the last 11 neckline increases will be worked as before in every 4th row. Only RS rows are written out. In all WS rows, work all sts as they appear (knitting the knits and purling the purls).

Rows 60, 64, 68, 72 (RS): Selv st, knit to 2nd marker, M1R from the bar between sts, slip m, k5, selv st.

Rows 61–63, 65–67, 69–71, 73–75: Work all sts as they appear (knitting the knits and purling the purls).

Row 76 (RS): Selv st, k5, slip m, M1L from the bar between sts, knit to 1 st before next m, M1R from the bar between sts, place m, k1, remove m, k4, selv st.

Row 78 (RS): Selv st, k5, slip m, M1L from the bar between sts, knit to end of row.

Row 80 (RS): Selv st, k5, slip m, M1L from the bar between sts, knit to m, M1R from the bar between sts, slip m, k5, selv st.

Rows 82, 86, 90, 94, 98 (RS): Work as Row 78.

Rows 84, 88, 92, 96, 100 (RS): Work as Row 80.

Size 5:

Armhole increases are to be worked in every other row (always in a RS row) a total of 15 times. At the same time, the last 11 neckline increases will be worked as before in every 4th row. Only RS rows are written out. In all WS rows, work all sts as they appear (knitting the knits and purling the purls).

Rows 60, 64, 68, 72, 76 (RS): Selv st, knit to 2nd marker, M1R from the bar between sts, slip m, k5, selv st.

Rows 61–63, 65–67, 69–71, 73–75, 77–79: Work all sts as they appear (knitting the knits and purling the purls).

Row 80 (RS): Selv st, k5, slip m, M1L from the bar between sts, knit to 1 st before next m, M1R from the bar between sts, place m, k1, remove m, k4, selv st.

Row 82 (RS): Selv st, k5, slip m, M1L from the bar between sts, knit to end of row.

Row 84 (RS): Selv st, k5, slip m, M1L from the bar between sts, knit to m, M1R from the bar between sts, slip m, k5, selv st.

Rows 86, 90, 94, 98, 102, 104, 106, 108 (RS): Work as Row 82.

Rows 88, 92, 96, 100 (RS): Work as Row 84.

Size 6:

Armhole increases are to be worked in every other row (always in a RS row) a total of 18 times. At the same time, the last 13 neckline increases will be worked as before in every 4th row. Only RS rows are written out. In all WS rows, work all sts as they appear (knitting the knits and purling the purls).

Rows 60, 64, 68, 72 (RS): Selv st, knit to 2nd marker, M1R from the bar between sts, slip m, k5, selv st.

Rows 61–63, 65–67, 69–71, 73–75: Work all sts as they appear (knitting the knits and purling the purls).

Row 76 (RS): Selv st, k5, slip m, M1L from the bar between sts, knit to 1 st before next m, M1R from the bar between sts, place m, k1, remove m, k4, selv st.

Row 78 (RS): Selv st, k5, slip m, M1L from the bar between sts, knit to end of row.

Row 80 (RS): Selv st, k5, slip m, M1L from the bar between sts, knit to m, M1R from the bar between sts, slip m, k5, selv st.

Rows 82, 86, 90, 94, 98, 102, 106, 110 (RS): Work as Row 78.

Rows 84, 88, 92, 96, 100, 104, 108 (RS): Work as Row 80.

Size 7:

Armhole increases are to be worked in every other row (always in a RS row) a total of 22 times. At the same time, the last 15 neckline increases will be worked as before in every 4th row. Only RS are written out. In all WS rows, work all sts as they appear (knitting the knits and purling the purls).

Rows 60, 64, 68, 72 (RS): Selv st, knit to 2nd marker, M1R from the bar between sts, slip m, k5, selv st.

Rows 61–63, 65–67, 69–71, 73–75: Work all sts as they appear (knitting the knits and purling the purls).

Row 76 (RS): Selv st, k5, slip m, M1L from the bar between sts, knit to 1 st before next m, M1R from the bar between sts, place m, k1, remove m, k4, selv st.

Row 78 (RS): Sclv st, k5, slip m, M1L from the bar between sts, knit to end of row.

Row 80 (RS): Selv st, k5, slip m, M1L from the bar between sts, knit to m, M1R from the bar between sts, slip m, k5, selv st.

Rows 82, 86, 90, 94, 98, 102, 106, 110, 114, 118 (RS): Work as Row 78.

Rows 84, 88, 92, 96, 100, 104, 108, 112, 116 (RS): Work as Row 80.

For all sizes:

All increases for V-neck and armhole have now been completed. You now have a total of 42/44/49/50/54/59/65 sts on the needles.

Body

Fronts and Back will now be joined.

Knit all 42/44/49/50/54/59/65 sts of the Upper Left Front, CO 4 new underarm sts, knit all 94/98/106/110/118/128/140 sts of the Upper Back, CO 4 new underarm sts, knit all 42/44/49/50/54/59/65 sts of the Upper Right Front. You now have a total of 186/194/212/218/234/254/278 sts on the needles.

Work in stockinette stitch in the round until the Body measures 18/18.5/19/19.25/19.75/20/20.5 in (46/47/48/49/50/51/52 cm) from cast-on edge, measured in the center Back.

Change to US 4 (3.5 mm) needles and work 2.25 in (6 cm) in 1 × 1 ribbing pattern. Bind off all sts using the Italian bind-off method (page 29).

Sleeves

At a rate of 1 st picked up from every 2 sts, pick up and knit 78/82/86/88/96/100/106 sts around the 1st armhole, beginning at the bottom of the armhole and working upward in the direction of the Shoulder. Join to work in the round and place a marker for the BoR. Place an additional marker after 39/41/43/44/48/50/53 sts for the Shoulder point.

First, work wrap and turn short rows (pages 14–15) to shape the Sleeve cap as follows:

Knit to Shoulder point marker, slip m, k7, turn work.

P7, slip m, p7, turn work.

Following the established sequence, work 8 more turns on each side, always working to 3 sts after the previous turn; the turning stitch of the previous row is always the 1st st of the 3 sts. Short rows for Sleeve cap shaping have now been completed.

Work in stockinette stitch in the round with Sleeve tapering decreases at the underside of the Sleeve, working decreases in every 8th/8th/8th/8th/7th/7th/6th rnd a total of 12/12/12/12/14/14/16 times. Work this **decrease round** as follows: K1, k2tog, k to last 3 sts, ssk, k1.

After having completed 12/12/12/12/14/14/16 decreases, a total of 96/96/96/96/98/98/96 rounds have been worked. The Sleeve has now reached a length of 12.5/12.5/12.5/12.5/13/13/12.5 in (32/32/32/32/33/33/32 cm). There are 54/58/62/64/68/72/74 sts on the needles.

Continue to work in stockinette stitch in the round until the Sleeve measures 15/15.25/15.75/16/16.5/17/17.25 in (38/39/40/41/42/43/44 cm) from the underarm. At this point, the Sleeve can be lengthened or shortened according to your personal preferences.

Change to US 6 (4.0 mm) needles and work 2.25 in (6 cm) in 1 × 1 ribbing. Bind off all sts using the Italian bind-off method (page 29).

Work the 2nd Sleeve the same way.

Button Band

Now pick up and knit a total of 319/327/333/341/347/355/365 sts along the front edge of the garment. Start at the bottom edge of the Right Front, work toward the top and back down along the Back. Pick up sts at a rate of 8 sts picked up from every 9 (picking up 1 st each from 8 consecutive sts and skipping the 9th st).

Please note that **selvedge stitches** will be worked differently on the Button Band: Knit the last st of every row, slip the 1st st of every row purlwise with yarn in front of work.

Work **Row 1 (WS)** as follows: Selv st, *p1, k1* to last 2 sts, p1, selv st.

Then work 4 rows in 1 × 1 ribbing, working all sts as they appear (knitting the knits and purling the purls).

Now work wrap and turn short rows (pages 14–15) for the Button Band:

RS Row: Work in 1 × 1 ribbing pattern (all sts as they appear) to last 91 sts, turn work.

WS Row: Work in 1 × 1 ribbing pattern (all sts as they appear) to last 91 sts, turn work.

RS Row: Work in 1 × 1 ribbing pattern (all sts as they appear) to last 111 sts, turn work.

WS Row: Work in 1 × 1 ribbing pattern (all sts as they appear) to last 111 sts, turn work.

RS Row: Work in 1 × 1 ribbing pattern (all sts as they appear) to last 131 sts, turn work.

WS Row: Work in 1 × 1 ribbing pattern (all sts as they appear) to last 131 sts, turn work.

RS Row: Work in 1 × 1 ribbing pattern (all sts as they appear) to end of row.

Work a WS row over all sts.

Now work the buttonholes as follows: Selv st, 2 sts in 1 × 1 ribbing as the sts appear, BO 3 sts, 22/22/21/21/21/21/20 sts in 1 × 1 ribbing as the sts appear, BO 3 sts, 22/22/21/21/21/21/20 sts in 1 × 1 ribbing as the sts appear, BO 3 sts, 22/22/21/21/21/21/20 sts in 1 × 1 ribbing as they appear, BO 3 sts, work remaining sts in 1 × 1 ribbing as they appear. In the following WS row, cast on 3 new sts each over every bound-off buttonhole, incorporating the newly cast-on sts into the 1 × 1 ribbing pattern. Work 4 rows more in 1 × 1 ribbing. Bind off all sts using the Italian bind-off method (page 29).

Finishing

Weave in all ends and attach 4 buttons to the Button Band opposite the buttonholes. Wash the cardigan in lukewarm water with a mild wool detergent. Block it spread out flat on an even, horizontal surface, and let it dry.

Chris

Beginning knitters who want to venture into new territory will find this beautiful turtleneck sweater the perfect opportunity. The stitch pattern of textured bands on the Front is composed of only knit and purl stitches and is quick and easy to work.

MATERIALS
· 1 strand Pascuali Alpaca Fino; DK/light worsted weight; 100% baby alpaca, 109 yds (100 m) per 1.75 oz (50 g); in 31 Ocher: 8/9/10/11/12/14/15 skeins
held together with
1 strand Pascuali Alpaca Lace; lace weight; 100% baby alpaca; 437 yds (400 m) per 1.75 oz (50 g); in 25 Mustard Brown: 2/3/3/3/3/4/4 skeins
· Total yardage required: 820/930/1,038/1,148/ 1,312/1,476/1,640 yds (750/850/950/1,050/1,200/ 1,350/1,500 m)
· Circular knitting needles in size US 7 (4.5 mm), 16 in (40 cm), 24 in (60 cm), 32 in (80 cm), and 40/ 48 in (100/120 cm) long
· Circular knitting needles in size US 6 (4.0 mm), 16 in (40 cm), and 32/40 in (80/100 cm) long
· DPN sets in size US 6 (4.0 mm) and US 7 (4.5 mm)
· Tapestry needle for weaving in ends
· Stitch markers

SIZES
1/2/3/4/5/6/7
Incorporated positive ease: 3.25–4.75 in (8–12 cm)
Chest circumference: 37.75/39.75/41.25/43.25/47.25/ 50.75/54.25 in (96/101/105/110/120/129/138 cm)
Upper arm circumference: 12.5/13.5/14.25/15/16/ 17.25/18.5 in (32/34/36/38/41/44/47 cm)
Length: 22/22.5/22.75/23.25/23.5/24/24.5 in (56/57/ 58/59/60/61/62 cm)
Our model wears size 4 (Women's L / Men's M)

GAUGE
17 sts and 26 rows = 4 × 4 inches (10 × 10 cm) in stockinette stitch with 1 strand of each yarn held together on US 7 (4.5 mm) needles (after washing and blocking)

STITCH PATTERNS
Textured Band Pattern on the Front in turned rows
Please refer to instructions within the pattern (page 48).

Textured Band Pattern on the Front in the round
Please refer to instructions within the pattern (page 49).

Shoulder/raglan stitches
Front and Sleeve as well as Back and Sleeve are separated by a 3-stitch-wide ribbing band. The stitches appear as "p1, k1, p1," and are always worked as they appear (knitting the knits and purling the purls). Next to these 3 sts, first Shoulder increases, then Sleeve increases, and finally, raglan increases, are worked. When the Sleeve stitches are placed on hold, these 3 sts will be reallocated to the Front and Back respectively.

Stockinette stitch for Sleeves and Back
Sleeves and Back are worked in stockinette stitch.
In rows: Knit on RS, purl on WS.
In rounds: Knit all stitches in all rounds.

1 × 1 ribbing for turtleneck collar and bottom edge
Alternate knit 1, purl 1.

CONSTRUCTION NOTES
The sweater is worked seamlessly in one piece from the top down, beginning at the turtleneck in 1 × 1 ribbing. The Yoke is worked next, first working short row shaping and at the same time the first of the Shoulder increases. Then Shoulder increases are finished in the round before Sleeve and raglan increases are worked. After the Sleeve stitches have been placed on hold, the Body is completed, then the Sleeves are worked in the round.
Work with 1 strand of each yarn held together throughout.

REGULAR FIT

LET'S START

Note: Work with 1 strand of each yarn held together throughout.

Yoke

Using US 6 (4.0 mm) needles, 16 in (40 cm) long, and a stretchy cast-on method, cast on 88/92/96/100/104/108/112 sts.

Join work into the round, taking care not to twist the cast-on row. Place a marker to indicate the BoR. The BoR is located in the center Back.

Work 7.5/7.5/8/8/8.25/8.25/8.75 in (19/19/20/20/21/21/22 cm) in 1 × 1 ribbing.

While working the last round, place markers to divide work into sections as follows:

Work 17/19/19/21/21/23/23 sts in ribbing (1st half of Back), place m, p1, k1, p1 (raglan sts), place m, 3 sts in ribbing (Sleeve), place m, p1, k1, p1 (raglan sts), place m, work 35/37/39/41/43/45/47 sts in ribbing (Front), place m, p1, k1, p1 (raglan sts), place m, 3 sts in ribbing (Sleeve), place m, p1, k1, p1 (raglan sts), place m, work 18/18/20/20/22/22/24 sts in 1 × 1 ribbing (2nd half of Back).

Front and Sleeve as well as Back and Sleeve are separated by a 3-stitch-wide ribbing band—the column of raglan line stitches. The stitches appear as "p1, k1, p1" and are always worked as they appear (knitting the knits and purling the purls). Next to these 3 sts, first Shoulder increases, then Sleeve increases, and finally raglan increases, are worked. When the Sleeve stitches are placed on hold, these 3 sts will be reallocated to the Front and Back respectively.

Change to US 7 (4.5 mm) needles. You will now work wrap and turn short rows (pages 14–15) to shape the neckline and at the same time begin to work Shoulder-shaping increases. Shoulder-shaping increases will be worked from here on in every row, a total of 10 times for each increase spot.

Textured Band Pattern on the Front in Rows

During the short rows for neckline shaping, the Textured Band Pattern on the Front will be worked first in turned rows. The pattern repeat has 10 rows heightwise, which are repeated continuously:

Rows 1–7 (RS): Alternate knit 1 row, purl 1 row.
Row 8 (WS): *P1, k1, repeat from * to end of row.

Row 9 (RS): *K1, p1, repeat from * to end of row.
Row 10 (WS): *P1, k1, repeat from * to end of row.

Row 1 (RS row, on the Front, Row 1 of the Textured Band Pattern is being worked): Knit to marker (Back), M1R from the bar between sts, slip m, p1, k1, p1, slip m, k3 (Sleeve), slip m, p1, k1, p1, slip m, M1L from the bar between sts (knitwise), k3, turn work.
Row 2 (WS row, on the Front, first Row 2, at the end Row 1 of the Textured Band pattern is being worked): Purl to marker, M1R-p from the bar between sts, slip m, k1, p1, k1, slip m, p3, slip m, k1, p1, k1, slip m, M1L-p from the bar between sts, purl to BoR marker, slip m, purl to next marker, M1R-p from the bar between sts, slip m, k1, p1, k1, slip m, p3, slip m, k1, p1, k1, slip m, M1L-p from the bar between sts, p3, turn work.

Row 3 (RS row, on the Front, Row 2 of the Textured Band Pattern is being worked): Knit to marker, M1R from the bar between sts, slip m, p1, k1, p1, slip m, k3 (Sleeve), slip m, p1, k1, p1, slip m, M1L from the bar between sts, knit to BoR marker.

You have now completed 1 turn on each side. On the Front, Rows 1 and 2 of the Textured Band Pattern have been worked respectively.

Complete 4 more turns on each side, always working to 3 sts after the previous turn. The turning stitch of the previous row will always be the 1st stitch of the 3 sts. Make sure to work the appropriate row of the Textured Band Pattern on the Front each time, following the written instructions of the pattern repeat as listed earlier.

Explained in detail:
At Turn #2, work Rows 3 and 4 of the Textured Band Pattern.
At Turn #3, work Rows 5 and 6 of the Textured Band Pattern.
At Turn #4, work Rows 7 and 8 of the Textured Band Pattern.
At Turn #5, work Rows 9 and 10 of the Textured Band Pattern.

You have now again reached the center Back and have, while working these short rows, already completed all 10 Shoulder increases for each increase spot. There are 128/132/136/140/144/148/152 sts on the needles: 55/57/59/61/63/65/67 sts each for Front and Back, 3 raglan sts each, and 3 Sleeve sts each.

Textured Band Pattern on the Front in Rounds
After having completed the short rows for neckline shaping, the Textured Band Pattern on the Front is worked in the round. The following 10 rounds will be continuously repeated heightwise:
Rnds 1–4: Knit all sts.
Rnds 5–7: Alternate purl 1 row, knit 1 row.
Rnds 8–10: *K1, p1, repeat from * to end of rnd.

From here on, continue in the round.
The Sleeves and the Back are worked in stockinette stitch, the 3 raglan sts are always worked as they appear (knitting the knits and purling the purls), and the Front is worked in Textured Band Pattern. When working the 1st round after having joined into the round, begin again with Rnd 1 of the Textured Band Pattern (see written-out instructions), and continue working the pattern repeat heightwise all the time.
At the same time, begin working Sleeve increases in every other round.
Work the following 2 rounds a total of 15/16/17/17/17/17/16 times:
Rnd 1: Knit to marker, slip m, p1, k1, p1, slip m, M1L from the bar between sts, knit to next m, M1R from the bar between sts, slip m, p1, k1, p1, slip m, work all Front sts according to the appropriate round of the pattern repeat, slip m, p1, k1, p1, slip m, M1L from the bar between sts, knit to next m, M1R from the bar between sts, slip m, p1, k1, p1, slip m, knit to BoR marker.
Rnd 2: Work all sts as they appear (knitting the knits and purling the purls), slipping all markers when you encounter them.

The Sleeve increases have now been completed. You have 188/196/204/208/212/216/216 sts on the needles: 55/57/59/61/63/65/67 sts each for Front and Back, 3 raglan sts each, and 33/35/37/37/37/37/35 sts each for the Sleeves.

From here on, regular raglan increases will be worked, likewise in every other round.
Work the following 2 rounds a total of 8/9/10/11/14/17/20 times:
Rnd 1: Knit to marker, M1R from the bar between sts, slip m, p1, k1, p1, slip m, M1L from the bar between sts, knit to next m, M1R from the bar between sts, slip m, p1, k1, p1, slip m, M1L from the bar between sts, work the Front sts according to the appropriate round of the pattern repeat to marker, M1R from the bar between sts, slip m, p1, k1, p1, slip m, M1L from the bar between sts, knit to next m, M1R from the bar between sts, slip m, p1, k1, p1, slip m, M1L from the bar between sts, knit to BoR marker.
Rnd 2: Work all sts as they appear (knitting the knits and purling the purls), slipping all markers when you encounter them.
All raglan increases have now been completed. You have 252/268/284/296/324/352/376 sts on the needles: 71/75/79/83/91/99/107 sts each for Front and Back, 3 raglan sts each, and 49/53/57/59/65/71/75 sts each for the Sleeves.

There are now 164/172/180/188/204/220/236 sts on the needles.

Work in the round, all sts as they appear (knitting the knits and purling the purls)—the sts of the Back in stockinette, 11 sts each at the side seam in 1 × 1 ribbing, the sts of the Front according to the appropriate row in the pattern repeat for the Textured Band Pattern—until the Body, measured from the highest point at the Shoulder, has reached a length of 19/19.25/19.75/20/20/20.75/21.25 in (48/49/50/51/51/53/54 cm). End with a Rnd 7 of the pattern repeat for the Front. Change to US 6 (4.0 mm) needles and work 3.1 in (8 cm) in 1 × 1 ribbing. Bind off all sts using the Italian bind-off method (page 29).

Sleeves

Take up the 49/53/57/59/64/71/75 previously held sts of the 1st Sleeve with a circular needle in size US 7 (4.5 mm), 16 in (40 cm) long, and pick up and knit 5 sts from the newly cast-on underarm stitches (= 54/58/62/64/70/76/80 sts). Place a marker for the BoR after 3 of the 5 sts.

Now work stockinette stitch in the round, at the same time working Sleeve tapering decreases at the underside of the Sleeve in every 14th/12th/10th/10th/8th/7th/6th rnd, a total of 6/7/8/8/10/12/13 times.

Work **Sleeve tapering decrease round** as follows: K1, ssk, k to last 3 sts, k2tog, k1.

After having completed 6/7/8/8/10/12/13 decreases, a total of 84/84/80/80/80/84/78 rounds have been worked. The Sleeve has now reached a length of 12.5/12.5/11.75/11.75/11.75/12.5/11.75 in (32/32/30/30/30/32/30 cm). You have a total of 42/44/46/48/50/52/54 sts on the needles.

Continue to work in stockinette stitch in the round until the Sleeve measures 15/15.25/15.75/16/16.5/17/17.25 in (38/39/40/41/42/43/44 cm) from the underarm. At this point, the Sleeve can be lengthened or shortened according to your personal preferences. Change to US 6 (4.0 mm) needles and work 2.25 in (6 cm) in 1 × 1 ribbing. Bind off all sts using the Italian bind-off method (page 29).

Work the 2nd Sleeve the same way.

Finishing

Weave in all ends and wash the sweater in lukewarm water with a mild wool detergent. Block it spread out flat on an even, horizontal surface, and let it dry.

Body

Sleeve stitches are now placed on hold. Raglan stitches are reallocated to the Body. They will be worked as established, including at the faux side seam on the Body, as they appear (knitting the knits and purling the purls). The newly cast-on underarm stitches will be incorporated into the ribbing pattern. This will create an 11-sts-wide strip in 1 × 1 ribbing at the side seam, which will be continued down to the bottom ribbing.

Knit to m, remove m, p1, k1, p1, transfer 49/53/57/59/65/71/75 sts to a spare cord or piece of waste yarn for holding, CO 5 new underarm sts, remove m, p1, k1, p1, remove m, work 71/75/79/83/91/99/107 sts according to the appropriate row of the pattern repeat for the Front to marker, remove m, p1, k1, p1, remove m, transfer 49/53/57/59/65/71/75 sts to a spare cord or piece of waste yarn for holding, CO 5 new underarm sts, remove m, p1, k1, p1, remove m, knit to end of round.

Robin

The ribbing of this turtleneck sweater's wide raglan lines progresses into decorative ribbed panels along the sides of the Body for a classic garment with a distinctive look. The luxurious lightweight yarn will keep you perfectly warm on cold fall and winter days.

MATERIALS

· Lamana Bergamo; worsted/Aran weight; 75% extra fine merino wool, 25% baby alpaca; 71 yds (65 m) per 0.9 oz (25 g) skein; in 58 Walnut: 13/ 14/17/19/22/25/28 skeins
  Total yardage required: 875/984/1,148/1,312/ 1,531/1,750/1,968.5 yds (800/900/1,050/1,200/ 1,400/1,600/1,800 m)
  Modifying the length of the garment will change the total yarn requirements accordingly.
· Circular knitting needles in size US 8 (5.0 mm), 16 in (40 cm), 24 in (60 cm), 32 in (80 cm), and 40/ 48 in (100/120 cm) long
· Circular knitting needles in size US 6 (4.0 mm), 16 in (40 cm) and 32/40 in (80/100 cm) long
· DPN sets in size US 6 (4.0 mm) and US 8 (5.0 mm)
· Tapestry needle for weaving in ends
· Stitch markers

SIZES

1/2/3/4/5/6/7
Incorporated positive ease: 4–7 in (10–18 cm)
Chest circumference: 37.5/39.25/41.75/44.5/46/50.5/ 54 in (95/100/106/113/117/128/137 cm)
Upper arm circumference: 12.5/13.5/13.75/15/16.25/ 17.25/19 in (32/34/35/38/41/44/48 cm)
Length: 21.25/21.75/22/22.75/23.25/23.5/24 in (54/ 55/56/58/59/60/61 cm)
Our model wears size 4 (Women's L / Men's M)

GAUGE

18 sts and 25 rows = 4 × 4 in (10 × 10 cm) in stockinette stitch on US 8 (5.0 mm) needles (after washing and blocking)

STITCH PATTERNS

2 × 2 ribbing for turtleneck collar, raglan lines, side panels, and bottom edge
Alternate knit 2, purl 2.

CONSTRUCTION NOTES

Work starts at the turtleneck, worked on a short circular needle in 2 × 2 ribbing in the round. After work has been divided into sections for raglan shaping, short rows are worked, then raglan increases are worked in the round. The wide raglan lines are worked in 2 × 2 ribbing, while Front, Back, and Sleeves are in stockinette stitch.
After Sleeve stitches have been placed on hold, the Body is finished in stockinette stitch in the round with decorative side panels in 2 × 2 ribbing slanting toward the Front. Sleeves are finished last, worked on a short circular needle in stockinette stitch in the round. The bottom edge of the Body as well as the Sleeve cuffs are worked in 2 × 2 ribbing.

Turtleneck Sweater with Ribbing Details

RELAXED FIT

LET'S START

Turtleneck

Using US 6 (4.0 mm) needles, 16 in (40 cm) long, and stretchy cast-on method, cast on 96/96/104/104/104/112/112 sts and join into the round, taking care not to twist the cast-on row. Place a marker to indicate the BoR. The BoR is located in the center Back. Work 7.5/7.5/8/8/8.25/8.25/8.75 in (19/19/20/20/21/21/22 cm) in 2 × 2 ribbing.

Divide the Yoke and Work Short Rows

Now, work a **setup round** in 2 × 2 ribbing, working all sts as they appear, placing 8 markers for raglan increases as follows:
Work 10/10/10/10/10/14/14 sts in 2 × 2 ribbing (Back), place m, work 10/10/10/10/10/10/10 sts in 2 × 2 ribbing (raglan sts), place m, work 10/10/10/10/10/10/10 sts in 2 × 2 ribbing (Sleeve), place m, work 10/10/10/10/10/10/10 sts in 2 × 2 ribbing (raglan sts), place m, 18/18/22/22/22/26/26 sts in 2 × 2 ribbing (Front), place m, work 10/10/10/10/10/10/10 sts in 2 × 2 ribbing (raglan sts), place m, work 10/10/10/10/10/10/10 sts in 2 × 2 ribbing (Sleeve), place m, work 10/10/10/10/10/10/10 sts in 2 × 2 ribbing (raglan sts), place m, 8/8/12/12/12/12/12 sts in 2 × 2 ribbing (Back). You have again reached the BoR in the center Back.

Now neckline shaping with wrap and turn short rows (pages 14–15) begins, while at the same time working raglan increases. Raglan increases are worked to the right of (before) and to the left of (after) the raglan line sts. Since Front, Back, and Sleeves are worked in stockinette stitch, all increased stitches are always knit. Change to US 8 (5.0 mm) needles.

Row 1 (RS): Knit to marker (Back), M1R from the bar between sts, slip m, work sts as they appear (knitting the knits and purling the purls) to marker (raglan sts), slip m, M1L from the bar between sts, knit to m (Sleeve), M1R from the bar between sts, slip m, work sts as they appear to marker (raglan sts), slip m, M1L from the bar between sts, k3, turn work.
Row 2 (WS): Work all sts as they appear to BoR marker, slipping all markers when you encounter them. Slip BoR marker, purl to m (Back), M1R from the bar between sts, slip m, work sts as they appear to marker (raglan sts), slip m, M1L from the bar between sts, purl to m (Sleeve), M1R from the bar between sts, slip

m, work sts as they appear to marker (raglan sts), slip m, M1L from the bar between sts, p3, turn work.
Row 3 (RS): Work all sts as they appear to BoR marker, slipping all markers when you encounter them.

You have now completed the 1st raglan increase for each increase spot and completed the 1st turn for each side (= 104/104/112/112/112/120/120 sts).
Repeat the 3 rows described above twice more, always working 3 sts past the previous turning spot.

You have now worked 3 raglan increases and 3 turns for each side. All short rows have been completed (= 120/120/128/128/128/136/136 sts).

Yoke

From here on, work in the round with raglan increases until you have worked a total of 21/23/24/27/29/32/36 increases for each increase spot. Raglan sts are worked as before in 2 × 2 ribbing as they appear; Front, Back and Sleeves are worked in stockinette stitch.

Now work the following 2 rounds a total of 18/20/21/24/26/29/33 times:
Rnd 1: Knit to marker (Back), M1R from the bar between sts, slip m, work sts as they appear (knitting the knits and purling the purls) to marker (raglan sts), slip m, M1L from the bar between sts, knit to m (Sleeve), M1R from the bar between sts, slip m, work sts as they appear to marker (raglan sts), slip m, M1L from the bar between sts, knit to m (Front), M1R from the bar between sts, slip m, work sts as they appear to marker (raglan sts), slip m, M1L from the bar between sts, knit to m (Sleeve), M1R from the bar between sts, slip m, work sts as they appear to marker (raglan sts), slip m, M1L from the bar between sts, knit to BoR marker, slip m.
Rnd 2: Work all sts as they appear, slipping all markers when you encounter them.
You have now completed a total of 21/23/24/27/29/32/36 raglan increases.
There are now 264/280/296/320/336/368/400 sts on the needles: 10/10/10/10/10/10/10 raglan sts each, 60/64/70/76/80/90/98 sts each for Front and Back, and 52/56/58/64/68/74/82 sts each for the Sleeves.
The Yoke has now been finished.

Body

Sleeve stitches are placed on hold and raglan stitches are reallocated to the Body:

Knit to marker, slip m, work sts as they appear (knitting the knits and purling the purls) to marker, remove m, place the following 52/56/58/64/68/74/82 sts on hold, CO 6 new underarm sts, remove m, work sts as they appear to marker, slip m, knit to m, slip m, work sts as they appear to marker, remove m, place the following 52/56/58/64/68/74/82 sts on hold, CO 6 new underarm sts, remove m, work sts as they appear to marker, slip m, knit to BoR marker, remove m, knit to m.

This marker will be the new BoR. There are 172/180/192/204/212/232/248 sts on the needles.

The 6 newly cast-on underarm sts on each side are incorporated into the 2 × 2 ribbing pattern and worked as k2, p2, k2. This creates side panels in 2 × 2 ribbing, each a total of 26 sts in width (= 10 raglan sts, 6 newly cast-on underarm sts, 10 raglan sts). These 26 sts on each side are framed by markers, 1 of these 4 markers is the marker for the BoR. Between the side markers, there are 60/64/70/76/80/90/98 sts each in stockinette stitch for Front and Back on the needles. Work in the round for 1.5 in (4 cm), working all sts as they appear (knitting the knits and purling the purls). Slip all markers as you encounter them.

Now, next to the side panels of 26 sts in 2 × 2 ribbing, decreases toward the Front and increases toward the Back will be worked. With every decrease worked, the Front becomes narrower, while with every increase worked, the Back becomes wider. This causes the ribbed side panels to visually travel to the Front in a diagonal direction.

Work the following 6 rounds a total of 11/11/10/11/11/10/10 times:

Rnd 1: M1R from the bar between sts, slip m, work 26 sts in 2 × 2 ribbing as they appear, slip m, ssk, knit to 2 sts before m, k2tog, slip m, work 26 sts in 2 × 2 ribbing as they appear, slip m, M1L from the bar between sts, knit to BoR marker.

Rnds 2–6: Work all sts as they appear, slipping all markers when you encounter them.

The Body has now reached a length of approximately 10.25/10.25/9.5/10.25/10.25/9.5/9.5 in (26/26/24/26/26/24/24 cm) from the held Sleeve stitches. The total length from the Shoulder is now about 18.5/19.25/18.5/20.5/21/21/21.75 in (47/49/47/52/53/53/55 cm). Continue to work in the round, working all sts as they appear, until the Body has reached a total length of 19/19.25/19.75/20.5/21/21.25/21.75 in (48/49/50/52/53/54/55 cm) from the Shoulder.

Change to US 6 (4.0 mm) needles and work 2.25 in (6 cm) in 2 × 2 ribbing, beginning with p2. Bind off all sts using a stretchy bind-off.

Sleeves

Take up the 52/56/58/64/68/74/82 previously held sts of the 1st Sleeve with a circular needle in size US 8 (5.0 mm), 16 in (40 cm) long, pick up and knit 6 sts from the newly cast-on Body sts (= 58/62/64/70/74/80/88 sts). Place a marker for the BoR after 3 of the 6 newly cast-on Body sts.

Now work stockinette stitch in the round, at the same time working Sleeve tapering decreases at the underside of the Sleeve in every 12th/12th/10th/9th/8th/7th/6th rnd a total of 7/7/8/9/11/12/16 times.

Work **Sleeve tapering decrease round** as follows: K1, ssk, k to last 3 sts, k2tog, k1.

After having completed 7/7/8/9/11/12/16 decreases, a total of 84/84/80/81/88/84/96 rounds have been worked. The Sleeve has now reached a length of 13.25/13.25/12.5/12.5/13.75/13/15 in (33.5/33.5/32/32/35/33/38 cm). There are 44/48/48/52/52/56/56 sts on the needles.

Continue to work in stockinette stitch in the round until the Sleeve measures 15/15.25/15.75/16.25/16.5/17/17.25 in (38/39/40/41/42/43/44 cm) from the underarm. At this point, the Sleeve can be lengthened or shortened according to your personal preferences. Change to US 6 (4.0 mm) needles and work 2.25 in (6 cm) in 2 × 2 ribbing. Bind off all sts using a stretchy bind-off.

Work the 2nd Sleeve the same way.

Finishing

Weave in all ends and wash the turtleneck sweater in lukewarm water with a mild wool detergent. Block it spread out flat on an even, horizontal surface, and let it dry.

Mika

I love stripes in all imaginable variations, widths, and colors. You can customize this simple vest, playing around with your favorite colors. Did I mention yet what a great project this would be for using up leftovers from your stash?

MATERIALS

· Lamana Como; DK weight; 100% extra fine merino wool; 131 yds (120 m) per 0.9 oz (25 g) skein: 6/6/7/7/8/8/9 total skeins
  Color combination 1 (shown on male model): 03 Silk Gray, 08 Curry, 48 Macadamia, 07 Khaki
  Color combination 2 (shown on female model): 03 Silk Gray, 40 Dusty Pink, 47 Nutmeg, 46 Basalt Blue
  Total yardage required: 711/765.5/820/875/930/1,038/1,148 yds (650/700/750/800/850/950/1,050 m)
· Circular knitting needles in size US 6 (4.0 mm), 24 in (60 cm), 32 in (80 cm), and 40/48 in (100/120 cm) long
· Circular knitting needles in size US 4 (3.5 mm), 16 in (40 cm) and 32/40 in (80/100 cm) long
· DPN set in size US 4 (3.5 mm)
· Tapestry needle for weaving in ends
· Stitch markers

SIZES

1/2/3/4/5/6/7
Incorporated positive ease: 2–3.25 in (5–8 cm)
Chest circumference: 35.75/37.75/40.5/43/45/48.75/52.25 in (91/96/103/109/114/124/133 cm)
Shoulder width: 13.5/13.75/14.25/14.5/15/15.25/15.75/16.25 in (34/35/36/37/38/39/40/41 cm)
Length: 21.25/21.75/22/22.5/22.75/23.25/23.5 in (54/55/56/57/58/59/60 cm)
Female model wears size 3 (Women's M/Men's S)
Male model wears size 5 (Women's XL/Men's L)

GAUGE

22 sts and 32 rows = 4 × 4 in (10 × 10 cm) in stockinette stitch on US 6 (4.0 mm) needles (after washing and blocking)

STITCH PATTERNS

Stockinette stitch in turned rows
RS Rows: Knit all stitches.
WS Rows: Purl all sts.

Stockinette stitch in the round
Knit all stitches.

Selvedge stitches
Knit all selvedge stitches in all RS and WS rows.

2 × 2 ribbing for bottom edge, Sleeve cuff, and collar
Alternate knit 2, purl 2.

CONSTRUCTION NOTES

Work starts with Shoulder increases worked in turned rows to create the Back and the 2 Fronts. At the same time, the neck opening is shaped, then the Fronts are joined, and the now-joined Front and the Back are continued separately to the armhole, while the Shoulder stitches are temporarily set aside.

After the Body has been joined into the round, it is continued in stockinette stitch in the round and finished with 2 × 2 ribbing. Finally, stitches are picked up around the neckline and armholes, and neckline and armhole finishing in 2 × 2 ribbing are added.

Vest with Color Block Pattern

REGULAR FIT

LET'S START

This design is worked with wide stripes, or color blocks. Each block is 24 rows or rounds in height, which equals about 3 in (7.5 cm). If you want your color blocks to look exactly as pictured, change color every 24 rows or rounds. If you want something different, plan your own from the endless possible stripe heights and color combinations.

Shoulders

Using US 6 (4.0 mm) needles, 24 in (60 cm) long, and a stretchy cast-on method, cast on 49/51/53/55/59/63/65 sts.

Row 1 is a WS row. Place 4 markers to divide the row into sections as follows: Selv st, p1 (Front), place m, p5 (Shoulder sts), place m, p35/37/39/41/45/49/51 (Back), place m, p5 (Shoulder sts), place m, p1 (Front), selv st. Now, immediately before and after the 5 Shoulder sts, increases will be worked in every row (RS and WS rows) 10/10/10/10/10/10/10 times. Work the following 2 rows a total of 5/5/5/5/5/5/5 times:

RS Row: Selv st, knit to m, M1R from the bar between sts, slip m, k5, slip m, M1L from the bar between sts, knit to m, M1R from the bar between sts, slip m, k5, slip m, M1L from the bar between sts, knit to last stitch, selv st.

WS Row: Selv st, purl to m, M1R from the bar between sts, slip m, p5, slip m, M1L from the bar between sts, purl to m, M1R from the bar between sts, slip m, p5, slip m, M1L from the bar between sts, purl to last stitch, selv st.

You have now completed 10/10/10/10/10/10/10 increase rows, while having increased 40/40/40/40/40/40/40 sts in all. There are 89/91/93/95/99/103/105 sts on the needles: 55/57/59/61/65/69/71 sts for the Back, 12/12/12/12/12/12/12 sts for each of the 2 Fronts, and 5 Shoulder sts on each side.

From here on, neckline increases will be additionally worked, 1st in every 4th row, then in every 2nd:

Row 1 (RS): Selv st, k5, M1L from the bar between sts, knit to m, M1R from the bar between sts, slip m, k5, slip m, M1L from the bar between sts, knit to m, M1R from the bar between sts, slip m, k5, slip m, M1L from the bar between sts, knit to last 6 sts, M1R from the bar between sts, k5, selv st.

Row 2 (WS): Selv st, purl to m, M1R from the bar between sts, slip m, p5, slip m, M1L from the bar between sts, purl to m, M1R from the bar between

sts, slip m, p5, slip m, M1L from the bar between sts, purl to last stitch, selv st.

Row 3 (RS): Selv st, knit to m, M1R from the bar between sts, slip m, k5, slip m, M1L from the bar between sts, knit to m, M1R from the bar between sts, slip m, k5, slip m, M1L from the bar between sts, knit to last stitch, selv st.

Row 4 (WS): Work as Row 2.

Row 5 (RS): Work as Row 1.

Row 6 (WS): Work as Row 2.

You have now completed 16 Shoulder increases for each increase spot and already worked 2 increases on each side at the neckline opening. There are 117/119/121/123/127/131/133 sts on the needles. Transfer the 67/69/71/73/77/81/83 sts of the Back and the 20 sts of the Right Front to a spare needle, extra cord, or piece of waste yarn for holding. Transfer the

5 Shoulder sts on each side to a separate safety pin for holding.

Left Front
First, work the 20 sts of the Left Front and complete neckline increases as follows:

Row 1 (RS): Selv st, knit to last stitch, selv st.
Row 2 (WS): Selv st, purl to last stitch, selv st.
Row 3 (RS): Selv st, k5, M1L from the bar between sts, knit to last stitch, selv st.
Row 4 (WS): Work as Row 2.
Row 5 (RS): Work as Row 1.
Row 6 (WS): Work as Row 2.
Repeat Rows 3 and 4 a total of 5/5/7/7/9/9/10 times. You should now have 26/26/28/28/30/30/31 sts on the needles.
Break the working yarn. Transfer the stitches to a spare needle, extra cord, or piece of waste yarn for holding.

Right Front
Place the 20 sts of the Right Front onto the needle again. Join new working yarn, and finish the increases here, too, as follows:

Row 1 (RS): Selv st, knit to last stitch, selv st.
Row 2 (WS): Selv st, purl to last stitch, selv st.
Row 3 (RS): Selv st, knit to last 6 sts, M1R from the bar between sts, k5, selv st.
Row 4 (WS): Work as Row 2.
Row 5 (RS): Work as Row 1.
Row 6 (WS): Work as Row 2.
Repeat Rows 3 and 4 a total of 5/5/7/7/9/9/10 times. There are 26/26/28/28/30/30/31 sts on the needles now.

Now, join the Right and the Left Front as follows:
RS Row: Knit all sts of the Right Front, knit the following 15/17/15/17/17/21/21 sts, knit all sts of the Left Front. You now have 67/69/71/73/77/81/83 sts on the needles.
WS Row: Selv st, purl to last stitch, selv st.
Now work 1.5/1.25/0.75/0.5/0.5/0.75/0 in (4/3.5/2/1.5/1.5/2/0 cm) in stockinette stitch in rows, ending with a WS row.
Work armhole increases in every other row, always in a RS row. Work the following 2 rows 11/13/16/18/19/22/26 times in all:
Row 1 (RS): Selv st, k5, M1L from the bar between sts, knit to last 6 sts, M1R from the bar between sts, k5, selv st.

Row 2 (WS): Selv st, purl to last stitch, selv st.
You now have 89/95/103/109/115/125/135 sts on the needles. Break the working yarn. Transfer the stitches to a spare needle, extra cord, or piece of waste yarn for holding.

Upper Back
Place the 67/69/71/73/77/81/83 sts of the Back onto the needle again. Join new working yarn and work 3.5/3.5/3.25/3.25/3.5/3.5/3.25 in (9/9/8/8/9/9/8 cm) in stockinette stitch in turned rows, ending with a WS row.
Work armhole increases in every other row, always in a RS row. Work the following 2 rows 11/13/16/18/19/22/26 times in all:
Row 1 (RS): Selv st, k5, M1L from the bar between sts, knit to last 6 sts, M1R from the bar between sts, k5, selv st.
Row 2 (WS): Selv st, purl to last stitch, selv st.
There are 89/95/103/109/115/125/135 sts on the needles now.

Body

Join to work in the round:

Knit all 89/95/103/109/115/125/135 sts of the Back, CO 11 new underarm sts, knit all 89/95/103/109/115/125/135 sts of the Right Front, CO 11 new underarm sts. Place a marker for the BoR after 5 of the 11 newly cast-on underarm sts. Work has been joined into the round. There are 200/212/228/240/252/272/292 sts on the needles.

Work in stockinette stitch in the round until the garment has reached a length of 18.5/19/19.25/19.75/20/20.5/20.75 in (47/48/49/50/51/52/53 cm) from Shoulder (transition to the neckline). Change to US 4 (3.5 mm) needles and work 2.75 in (7 cm) in 2 × 2 ribbing. Bind off all sts using a stretchy bind-off.

Armhole Ribbing

Using US 4 (3.5 mm) needles, 16 in (40 cm) long, for armhole ribbing, pick up about 116/124/128/132/144/156/160 sts, evenly distributed, around the armhole at a ratio of 8 sts picked up from every 9 sts (picking up 8 consecutive sts and skipping the 9th).

Begin at the underarm, in the middle of the newly cast-on underarm sts of the Body, and work upward in the direction of the Shoulder. When you have reached the Shoulder, incorporate the 5 formerly held sts from the safety pin into the pattern, carrying the working yarn loosely in back of work across these 5 sts. Continue on the other side in the direction of the armhole. Should you have picked up a different number of stitches than listed, make sure your stitch count is a multiple of 4. Join to work in the round. Place a marker to indicate the BoR.

Now, work 1.25 in (3 cm) in 2 × 2 ribbing. Bind off all sts using a stretchy bind-off.

Neckband

Using US 4 (3.5 mm) needles, 16 in (40 cm) long, pick up a total of 96/96/100/104/112/120/120 sts around the neckline edge at a ratio of 8 sts picked up from every 9 sts. Begin in the center Back and work your way around the neckline evenly spaced. Should you have picked up a different number of stitches than listed, make sure your stitch count is a multiple of 4. Join to work in the round. Place a marker to indicate the BoR. Now, work 1 round in 2 × 2 ribbing, setting up the ribbing pattern.

Then work wrap and turn short rows (pages 14–15) as follows:

RS Row: Work 44 sts in 2 × 2 ribbing as the sts appear, turn work.

WS Row: Work 88 sts in 2 × 2 ribbing as the sts appear, turn work.

RS Row: Work 78 sts in 2 × 2 ribbing as the sts appear, turn work.

WS Row: Work 68 sts in 2 × 2 ribbing as the sts appear, turn work.

RS Row: Work 58 sts in 2 × 2 ribbing as the sts appear, turn work.

WS Row: Work 48 sts in 2 × 2 ribbing as the sts appear, turn work.

RS Row: Work 38 sts in 2 × 2 ribbing as the sts appear, turn work.

WS Row: Work 28 sts in 2 × 2 ribbing as the sts appear, turn work.

Work 10 rounds in 2 × 2 ribbing, working all sts as they appear.

Purl 1 round (fold line).

Work 10 rounds in 2 × 2 ribbing, working all sts as they appear.

RS Row: Work 14 sts in 2 × 2 ribbing as the sts appear, turn work.

WS Row: Work 28 sts 2 × 2 ribbing as the sts appear, turn work.

RS Row: Work 38 sts in 2 × 2 ribbing as the sts appear, turn work.

WS Row: Work 48 sts in 2 × 2 ribbing as the sts appear, turn work.

RS Row: Work 58 sts in 2 × 2 ribbing as the sts appear, turn work.

WS Row: Work 68 sts in 2 × 2 ribbing as the sts appear, turn work.

RS Row: Work 78 sts in 2 × 2 ribbing as the sts appear, turn work.

WS Row: Work 88 sts in 2 × 2 ribbing as the sts appear, turn work.

Work 1 round in 2 × 2 ribbing, working all sts as they appear.

Bind off all sts using a stretchy bind-off.

Finishing

Weave in all ends. Fold the neckband along the fold line and sew it on around the pick-up edge with small, neat stitches. Wash your vest in lukewarm water with a mild wool detergent. Block it spread out flat on an even, horizontal surface, and let it dry.

Max

Another one of my favorites . . . I'm really fond of Max! Thanks to the sleek V-neck, the smart shoulder construction, and the contemporary turn-up at the sleeve, this sweater is amazingly versatile. I can imagine it looking quite nice in a striped pattern, too, like a classic blue-and-white combination!

MATERIALS
· Pascuali Pinta, held double; fingering/sock weight; 60% extra fine merino wool, 20% silk, 20% ramie; 232 yds (212 m) per 1.75 oz (50 g) skein; in 10 Khaki: 4/4/5/5/5/7/8 skeins
Total yardage required: 711/820/984/1,148/1,258/ 1,422/1,640 yds (650/750/900/1,050/1,150/1,300/ 1,500 m)
Modifying the length of the garment will change the total yarn requirements accordingly.
· Circular knitting needles in size US 7 (4.5 mm), 16 in (40 cm), 24 in (60 cm), 32 in (80 cm), and 40/ 48 in (100/120 cm) long
· Circular knitting needles in size US 6 (4.0 mm), 32 in (80 cm) and 40 in (100 cm) long
· DPN sets in sizes US 6 (4.0 mm) and US 7 (4.5 mm)
· 2 buttons, 0.6 in (15 mm) diameter
· Tapestry needle for weaving in ends
· Stitch markers

SIZES
1/2/3/4/5/6/7
Incorporated positive ease: 4–7 in (10–18 cm)
Chest circumference: 37.5/38.5/40.5/43.25/45.75/50/ 54.75 in (95/98/103/110/116/127/139 cm)
Upper arm circumference: 13/13.75/14.25/15/16.25/ 17.25/19.25 in (33/35/36/38/41/44/49 cm)
Length: 21.75/22/22.5/22.75/23.25/23.5/24 in (55/ 56/57/58/59/60/61 cm)
Our model wears size 4 (Women's L / Men's M)

GAUGE
18 sts and 26 rows = 4 × 4 inches (10 × 10 cm) with 2 strands of yarn held together in stockinette stitch on US 7 (4.5 mm) needles (after washing and blocking)

STITCH PATTERNS
Stockinette stitch in turned rows
RS Rows: Knit all stitches.
WS Rows: Purl all sts.

Stockinette stitch in the round
Knit all stitches.

Selvedge stitches
Knit all selvedge stitches in all RS and WS rows (knotted selvedge).

CONSTRUCTION NOTES
Work starts at the top of the Back, first working Shoulder increases then armhole increases, after which the stitches of the Upper Back are placed on hold. Then stitches are picked up for the Left Front and Right Front, and armhole and V-neck are shaped with increases and decreases. After this, both halves of the Front and the Back are joined, and the Body is completed in stockinette stitch in the round. The bottom is finished with a rolled edge worked on smaller needles. Then Sleeve stitches are picked up around the armhole, the Sleeve cap is shaped with short rows, and the Sleeve worked in stockinette stitch in the round. As a final touch, a buttoned strap is attached to the inside of the Sleeve.
Work with 2 strands of yarn held together throughout.

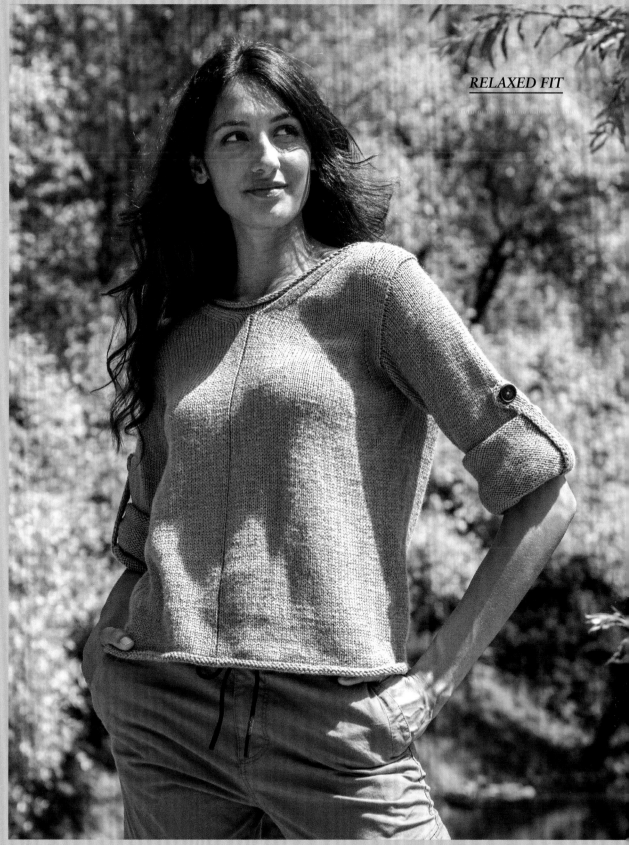

Sweater with V-neck and Turned-up Sleeves

RELAXED FIT

63

LET'S START

Upper Back

With 2 strands of yarn held together, US 7 (4.5 mm) needles, 24 in (60 cm) long and stretchy cast-on method, cast on 39/41/43/45/47/49/51 sts.

Row 1 is a WS row. Place 2 markers as follows: Selv st, p5, place m, purl to last 6 sts, place m, p5, selv st. From here on, increases will be worked in every row (RS and WS rows) immediately adjacent to the markers. Work the following 2 rows 9/9/9/10/10/11/12 times in all:

RS Row: Selv st, k5, slip m, M1L from the bar between sts, knit to m, M1R from the bar between sts, slip m, k5, selv st.

WS Row: Selv st, p5, slip m, M1L from the bar between sts, purl to m, M1R from the bar between sts, slip m, p5, selv st.

You have now completed 18/18/18/20/20/22/24 increases on each side. There are 75/77/79/85/87/93/99 sts on the needles.

Work 3.25/3.25/3.25/2.75/2/1.25/1.25 in (8/8/8/7/5/3/3 cm) in stockinette stitch in turned rows, ending with a WS row.

Now armhole increases will be worked in every other row, always in a RS row. Work the following 2 rows 10/11/11/12/15/18/22 times in all:

RS Row: Selv st, k5, slip m, M1L from the bar between sts, knit to m, M1R from the bar between sts, slip m, k5, selv st.

WS Row: Work all sts as they appear (knitting the knits and purling the purls), slipping all markers when you encounter them.

You now have 95/99/101/109/117/129/143 sts on the needles. Break the working yarn and transfer these stitches to a piece of waste yarn, an extra needle, or a spare cord for holding.

Upper Left Front

For this part, pick up and knit 18/18/18/20/20/22/24 sts from the slanted part of the Back Left Shoulder. Begin picking up at the neckline opening and pick up 1 st from each selvedge stitch of the Back. Finish picking up at the Shoulder point of the armhole.

Row 1 is a WS row. Place 2 markers as follows: Selv st, p4, place m, purl to last 6 sts, place m, p5, selv st. From here on V-neck shaping increases will be worked at the right edge of the Left Front in every other row (always in a RS row), 19/20/21/22/23/24/25 times in all.

At the same time, decreases will be worked at the left edge of the Left Front in every 6th row (always in a RS row) 4 times in all. Please note that only RS rows are written out in the following instructions. In all WS rows, work all sts as they appear (knitting the knits and purling the purls).

Rows 2, 4: Selv st, k5, slip m, M1L from the bar between sts, knit to end of row.

Row 6: Selv st, k5, slip m, M1L from the bar between sts, knit to 2 sts before the 2nd marker, k2tog, slip m, k4, selv st.

Rows 8, 10, 14, 16, 20, 22: Work as Row 2.

Row 12, 18, 24: Work as Row 6.

All decreases on the Shoulder side have now been completed. Remove the marker for the Shoulder side decreases.

You have worked 12 V-neck increases so far. There are 26/26/26/28/28/30/32 sts on the needles.

Work the following 2 rows 7/8/9/10/11/12/13 times to complete the neckline increases:

RS Row: Selv st, k5, slip m, M1L from the bar between sts, knit to end of row.

WS Row: Work all sts as they appear (knitting the knits and purling the purls).

You have now completed a total of 19/20/21/22/23/24/25 increases at the neck side. There are 33/34/35/38/39/42/45 sts on the needles. Break the working yarn and set these stitches temporarily aside on a spare needle or cord.

Upper Right Front

For this part, pick up and knit 18/18/18/20/20/22/24 sts from the slanted part of the Back Right Shoulder. Begin picking up at the Shoulder point of the armhole and pick up 1 st from each selvedge stitch of the Back. Finish picking up at the neckline opening.

Row 1 is a WS row. Place 2 markers as follows: Selv st, p5, place m, purl to last 5 sts, place m, p4, selv st. From here on, V-neck shaping increases will be worked at the left edge of the Right Front in every other row (always in a RS row), 19/20/21/22/23/24/25 times in all. At the same time, decreases will be worked at the right edge of the Right Front in every 6th row (always in a RS row), 4 times in all. Please note that only RS rows are written out in the following instructions. In all WS rows, work all sts as they appear (knitting the knits and purling the purls).

Rows 2, 4: Selv st, knit to 2nd marker, M1R from the bar between sts, slip m, k5, selv st.

Row 6: Selv st, k4, slip m, ssk, knit to m, M1R from the bar between sts, slip m, k5, selv st.

Rows 8, 10, 14, 16, 20, 22, 24: Work as Row 2.

Row 12, 18: Work as Row 6.

All decreases on the Shoulder side have now been completed. Remove the marker for the Shoulder side decreases.

You have worked 12 V-neck increases so far. There are 26/26/26/28/28/30/32 sts on the needles.

Work the following 2 rows 7/8/9/10/11/12/13 times to complete the neckline increases:

RS Row: Selv st, knit to 2nd marker, M1R from the bar between sts, slip m, k5, selv st.

WS Row: Work all sts as they appear (knitting the knits and purling the purls).

Now the Right and Left Front will be joined as follows:

Knit all sts of the Right Front, CO 1 new underarm st, continue by knitting the formerly held sts of the Left Front. You now have a total of 67/69/71/77/79/85/91 sts on the needles. Please note that the newly cast-on stitch in the Center Front should appear as a purl stitch on the RS of the knitted fabric. This means that this stitch is to be purled in RS rows and knitted in WS rows. When you work in the round later, this stitch will be purled in all rounds.

Therefore, now work a WS row over all sts as they appear (knitting the knits and purling the purls and knitting the newly cast-on center stitch).

Now, begin to work armhole increases. Work the following 2 rows 10/11/11/12/15/18/22 times in all:

RS Row: Selv st, k5, M1L from the bar between sts, work all sts as they appear (knitting the knits, purling the purls, and purling the center stitch) to last 6 sts, M1R from the bar between sts, k5, selv st.

WS Row: Work all sts as they appear (knitting the knits, purling the purls, and knitting the center stitch). You should now have a total of 87/91/93/101/109/121/135 sts on the needles.

Body

Now the Body is joined into the round: Work all sts of the Front as they appear (knitting the knits and purling the purls), CO 4/5/6/6/7/8/8 new underarm sts, work all sts of the Back as they appear, CO 4/5/6/6/7/8/8 new underarm sts, and join to work in the round. Place a marker for the BoR after 2/2/3/3/3/4/4 of the newly cast-on sts.

Work in stockinette stitch in the round (purling the center stitch), until your sweater measures approximately 21.25/21.75/22/22.5/22.75/23.25/23.5 in (54/55/56/57/58/59/60 cm) from the highest point at the Shoulder. Change to US 6 (4.0 mm) needles and, for the rolled edge, knit 6 rounds, including the center stitch. Bind off all sts using a stretchy bind-off.

Sleeves

Pick up and knit a total of 60/64/66/68/74/80/88 stitches around the 1st armhole at a rate of 1 st picked up from every 2 sts. Begin picking up in the center of the underarm sts and work upward over the Shoulder and back down again to the underarm. Join to work in the round and place a marker for the BoR. Place an additional marker for the highest point at the Shoulder after 30/32/33/34/37/40/44 sts.

Then work wrap and turn short rows (pages 14–15) to shape the Sleeve cap as follows:

Knit to Shoulder point marker, slip m, k7, turn work. P7, slip m, p7, turn work.

Following the established sequence, work 5 more turns on each side, always working to 3 sts after the previous turn; the turning stitch of the previous row is always the 1st stitch of the 3 sts.

Short rows for Sleeve cap shaping have now been completed.

Work in stockinette stitch in the round until the Sleeve measures 4/4.25/4.25/4.75/4.75/4.75/5 in (10/11/11/12/12/12/13 cm) from the armhole.

At this point, mark the position for the button strap in the upper part of the Sleeve as follows: Knit to 3 sts before the Shoulder point marker, p7, knit the remaining sts of the round.

Work 6 more rounds in stockinette with these 7 sts purled (as they appear).

After having completed these rounds, continue in regular stockinette stitch in the round until the Sleeve measures approximately 15.75/16.25/16.5/17/17.25/17.75/18 in (40/41/42/43/44/45/46 cm) from the armhole. Change to US 6 (4.0 mm) needles and, for the rolled edge, work 6 rounds in stockinette stitch. Bind off all sts using a stretchy bind-off.

Work the 2nd Sleeve the same way.

Rolled Neckline Edge
Using circular knitting needles in size US 6 (4.0 mm), 16 in (40 cm) long, pick up stitches around the neckline edge. Begin in the center Back, picking up a total of 69/73/76/80/84/87/90 sts at a ratio of 8 sts picked up from every 9 sts. Join to work in the round and place a marker for the BoR. Work 6 rounds in stockinette stitch. Bind off all sts using a stretchy bind-off.

Turn-up Button Strap at the Sleeve (pictured at left)
Turn your sweater inside out. Take up the 1st Sleeve and, using US 6 (4.0 mm) needles, pick up a total of 9 sts at the top edge of the purled rectangle. Pick up 1 st before the rectangle, pick up all 7 sts of the rectangle, and pick up 1 st after the rectangle.

The last stitch of every row will be knitted. The 1st stitch of every row will be slipped purlwise with yarn in front of work.

Join new working yarn and work **Row 1 (WS row)** as follows: Selv st, p1, k1 to last 2 sts, p1, selv st.

Work in turned rows, all sts as they appear (knitting the knits and purling the purls), until the strap has reached a length of 11.75/11.75/12.5/12.5/12.5/13.5/13.5 in (30/30/32/32/32/34/34 cm), ending with a WS row.

Work a buttonhole: Selv st, k1, p1, k1, k2tog, 1 yo, p1, k1, selv st.

Work all sts as they appear (knitting the knits and purling the purls) for another 0.5 in (1.5 cm), then bind off all sts using a stretchy bind-off.

Work the 2nd strap the same way.

Finishing
Weave in all ends and wash your sweater in lukewarm water with a mild wool detergent. Block it spread out flat on an even, horizontal surface, and let it dry. Attach 1 button each at the reverse stockinette rectangles in the upper part of the Sleeves, going through both the fabric of the Sleeve and the fabric of the strip for reinforcement when sewing on the button.

Andy

This varsity-style jacket with contrasting color sleeves and inset side pockets with plackets may be one of the more complicated projects, but it's certainly also one of the most eye-catching designs! It looks best when simply combined with white shirt, jeans, and sneakers.

MATERIALS

· *For the Body:* Lang Yarns Merino +; worsted weight; 100% extra fine merino wool; 98.5 yds (90 m) per 1.75 oz (50 g); in 152.0035 Marine: 7/7/9/10/11/12/13 skeins

For the Sleeves: Lang Yarns Merino +; worsted weight; 100% extra fine merino wool; 98.5 yds (90 m) per 1.75 oz (50 g); in 152.0063 Dark Red: 5/5/6/6/7/7/8 skeins

Total yardage required: 1,039/1,148/1,312/1,476/1,640/1,804.5/1,968.5 yds (950/1,050/1,200/1,350/1,500/1,650/1,800 m) for the whole jacket, of these about 437.5/492/546.8/546.8/601.5/656/711 yds (400/450/500/500/550/600/650 m) for the Sleeves

· Circular knitting needles in size US 7 (4.5 mm), 16 in (40 cm), 24 in (60 cm), 32 in (80 cm), and 40/48 in (100/120 cm) long
· Circular knitting needles in size US 6 (4.0 mm), 32 in (80 cm) and 40 in (100 cm) long
· DPN sets in size US 6 (4.0 mm) and US 7 (4.5 mm)
· 5 sew-on metal snaps, 0.8–0.9 in (21–24 mm) diameter, and sewing thread in a matching color
· Tapestry needle for weaving in ends
· Stitch markers

SIZES

1/2/3/4/5/6/7

Incorporated positive ease: 3.25–4.75 in (8–12 cm)
Chest circumference: 36.5/38.25/40.5/42.5/45.75/47.25/53.5 in (93/97/103/108/116/125/136 cm)
Upper arm circumference: 16.5/17/17.75/18/19/21/22 in (42/43/45/46/48/53/56 cm)
Length: 21/21/22/22/22.75/23.25/23.25 in (53/53/56/56/58/59/59 cm)
Our model wears size 3 (Women's M / Men's S)

GAUGE

18 sts and 26 rows = 4 × 4 inches (10 × 10 cm) in stockinette stitch on US 7 (4.5 mm) needles (after washing and blocking)

STITCH PATTERNS

Stockinette stitch in turned rows
RS Rows: Knit all stitches.
WS Rows: Purl all sts.

Stockinette stitch in the round
Knit all stitches.

1 × 1 ribbing for Collar, Button Band, Pocket Plackets, and bottom ribbing
Alternate knit 1, purl 1.

Selvedge stitches
In the Body, selvedge stitches in all RS and WS rows are knitted. In the Button Bands and the Pocket Plackets, the last stitch of every row is knitted, the 1st stitch of every row is slipped purlwise with yarn in front of work.

CONSTRUCTION NOTES

First, the Upper Back is shaped with Shoulder and armhole increases, then both Fronts are knitted onto the existing piece. Under the arm, the Body is joined into the round and worked in stockinette stitch up to the Pocket Openings. After having completed the Pocket Openings, the Body is finished with 1 × 1 ribbing. Sleeve stitches are picked up in a contrasting color, the Sleeve cap is shaped, and the Sleeves are knit in stockinette stitch in the round with a 1 × 1 ribbed cuff. Finally, Collar and Button Band as well as the Pocket Plackets and Pocket Linings are worked in 1 × 1 ribbing.

REGULAR FIT

LET'S START

Upper Back

Using US 7 (4.5 mm) needles, 24 in (60 cm) long, and a stretchy cast-on method, cast on 29/31/33/35/37/39/41 sts.

Row 1 is a WS row. Place 2 markers as follows: Selv st, p5, place m, purl to last 6 sts, place m, p5, selv st. From here on, increases will be worked in every row (RS and WS rows) immediately adjacent to the markers. Work the following 2 rows 10/10/11/11/12/12/13 times:

RS Row: Selv st, k5, slip m, M1L from the bar between sts, knit to m, M1R from the bar between sts, slip m, k5, selv st.

WS Row: Selv st, p5, slip m, M1L from the bar between sts, purl to m, M1R from the bar between sts, slip m, p5, selv st.

You have now increased 20/20/22/22/24/24/25 sts on each side. There are 69/71/77/79/85/87/93 sts on the needles.

Work 2.75 in (7 cm) in stockinette stitch in turned rows, ending with a WS row.

Armhole increases will be worked in every other row, always in a RS row.

Work the following 2 rows 9/10/10/11/12/15/17 times:

RS Row: Selv st, k5, slip m, M1L from the bar between sts, knit to m, M1R from the bar between sts, slip m, k5, selv st.

WS Row: Work all sts as they appear (knitting the knits and purling the purls), slipping all markers when you encounter them.

You should now have 87/91/97/101/109/117/127 sts on the needles. Break the working yarn and transfer these stitches to a piece of waste yarn, an extra needle, or a spare cord for holding.

Upper Right Front

For the Right Front, pick up and knit 21/21/23/23/25/25/27 sts from the slanted part of the Back Right Shoulder. Begin picking up at the Shoulder point of the armhole and pick up 1 st from each selvedge stitch of the Back. Finish picking up at the neckline edge.

Row 1 is a WS row. Place 2 markers as follows: Selv st, p5, place m, purl to last 5 sts, place m, p4, selv st. From here on, you will at the same time work decreases at the right edge to make the Shoulders narrower, as well as neckline shaping increases at the left edge.

In the following instructions, only RS rows are writ-

ten out. In all WS rows, all stitches are worked as they appear (knitting the knits and purling the purls).

Rows 2, 4: Work all sts as they appear (knitting the knits and purling the purls).

Row 6: Selv st, k4, slip m, ssk, knit to end of row.

Rows 8, 10: Work as Row 4.

Row 12: Selv st, k4, slip m, ssk, knit to next m, M1R from the bar between sts, slip m, k5, selv st.

Row 14: Work as Row 2.

Row 16: Selv st, knit to 2nd marker, M1R from the bar between sts, slip m, k5, selv st.

Row 18: Work as Row 6.

Rows 20, 22, 26, 28, 32, 34: Work as Row 16.

Rows 24, 30, 36: Work as Row 12.

All decreases on the Shoulder side have now been completed, and the marker for the Shoulder increases may be removed. Up to this point, 11 increases at the neck side have been worked. Repeat the following 2 rows 0/0/0/0/1/2/3 time(s):

Row 1 (RS): Selv st, knit to 2nd marker, M1R from the bar between sts, slip m, k5, selv st.

Row 2 (WS): Work all sts as they appear (knitting the knits and purling the purls).

Neckline increases for all sizes have now been completed. There are 26/26/28/28/31/32/35 sts on the needles.

Work a RS row over all stitches. At the end of the row, cast on an additional 3 sts to extend the row (= 29/29/31/31/34/35/38 sts).

Work 2 in (5 cm) in stockinette stitch in turned rows, ending with a WS row.

Begin to work the armhole increases. Increases will be worked in every other row, always in a RS row.

Work the following 2 rows 9/10/10/11/12/15/17 times:

Row 1 (RS): Selv st, k5, M1L from the bar between sts, knit to end of row.

Row 2 (WS): Work all sts as they appear (knitting the knits and purling the purls).

Armhole increases have now been completed. There are 38/39/41/42/46/50/55 sts on the needles.

Break the working yarn and transfer these stitches to a piece of waste yarn, an extra needle, or a spare cord for holding.

Upper Left Front

For the Left Front, pick up and knit 21/21/23/23/25/25/27 sts from the slanted part of the Back Left Shoulder. Begin picking up at the neckline opening and pick up 1 st from each selvedge stitch of the Back. Finish picking up at the Shoulder point of the armhole.

Row 1 is a WS row. Place 2 markers as follows: Selv st, p4, place m, purl to last 6 sts, place m, p5, selv st. From here on, you will at the same time work decreases at the left edge to make the Shoulders narrower, as well as neckline shaping increases at the right edge. In the following instructions, only RS rows are written out. In all WS rows, all stitches are worked as they appear (knitting the knits and purling the purls).

Rows 2, 4: Work all sts as they appear (knitting the knits and purling the purls).
Row 6: Selv st, knit to 2 sts before the 2nd marker, k2tog, slip m, k4, selv st.
Rows 8, 10: Work as Row 4.
Row 12: Selv st, k5, slip m, M1L from the bar between sts, knit to 2 sts before m, k2tog, slip m, k4, selv st.
Row 14: Work as Row 2.
Row 16: Selv st, k5, slip m, M1L from the bar between sts, knit to end of row.
Row 18: Work as Row 6.
Rows 20, 22, 26, 28, 32, 34: Work as Row 16.
Row 24, 30, 36: Work as Row 12.

All decreases on the Shoulder side have now been completed, and the marker for the Shoulder increases may be removed. Up to this point, 11 increases at the neck side have been worked.
Work the following 2 rows 0/0/0/0/1/2/3 time(s):
Row 1 (RS): Selv st, k5, slip m, M1L from the bar between sts, knit to end of row.
Row 2 (WS): Work all sts as they appear (knitting the knits and purling the purls).
Neckline increases for all sizes have now been completed. There are 26/26/28/28/31/32/35 sts on the needles.

Before the beginning of the next row, cast on an additional 3 sts to extend the row, then knit all stitches of the next RS row including the 3 newly cast-on sts (= 29/29/31/31/34/35/38 sts).
Work 2 in (5 cm) in stockinette stitch in turned rows, ending with a WS row.
Begin to work the armhole increases. Increases will be worked in every other row, always in a RS row.
Work the following 2 rows 9/10/10/11/12/15/17 times:
Row 1 (RS): Selv st, knit to last 6 sts, M1R from the bar between sts, k5, selv st.

Row 2 (WS): Work all sts as they appear (knitting the knits and purling the purls).
Armhole increases have now been completed. There are 38/39/41/42/46/50/55 sts on the needles.

Body
Now all separately worked pieces will be joined.
Knit all 38/39/41/42/46/50/55 sts of the Left Front, CO 4 new underarm sts, knit all 87/91/97/101/109/117/127 sts of the Back, CO 4 new underarm sts, knit all 38/39/41/42/46/50/55 sts of the Right Front.
You should now have 171/177/187/193/209/225/245 sts for the Body on the needles.
Work in stockinette stitch in turned rows until the piece measures approximately 14.25/14.25/15/15/15.75/15.75/15.75 in (36/36/38/38/40/40/40 cm) from the highest point at the Shoulder, ending with a WS row. Now Pocket Openings will be incorporated.

Pocket Openings
For this part, divide work into 3 sections to be worked separately: the Left Front, the Right Front, and the combined Sides/Back. Begin at the Left Front edge and k20/20/22/22/22/24/24, kfb, and turn work. Using a spare needle, work a WS row over all stitches. You now have 22/22/24/24/24/26/26 sts on a separate needle. The remaining stitches (150/156/164/170/186/200/220) are being temporarily set aside.
Over the 22/22/24/24/24/26/26 sts from the separate needle, work 4/4/4.25/4.25/4.25/4.75/4.75 in (10/10/11/11/11/12/12 cm) in stockinette stitch in turned rows, ending this part with a WS row. Transfer the stitches to a spare needle, extra cord, or piece of waste yarn for holding.
Now complete the combined Sides/Back as follows: Join new working yarn and, beginning with a RS row over the previously held stitches, kfb, k127/133/139/145/161/173/193 sts, kfb, and turn work. Take up another spare needle and work a WS row over the just-worked stitches. On this new needle, you now have 131/137/143/149/165/177/197 sts. Over these sts, now likewise work 4/4/4.25/4.25/4.25/4.75/4.75 in (10/10/11/11/11/12/12 cm) in stockinette stitch in turned rows, ending with a WS row. Transfer the stitches to a spare needle, extra cord, or piece of waste yarn for holding.

Complete the Right Front as follows: Join new working yarn and work a RS row over the remaining previously held stitches, kfb, then k20/20/22/22/22/24/24. There are 22/22/24/24/24/26/26 sts on the needles. Over these sts, now likewise work 4/4/4.25/4.25/4.25/4.75/4.75 in (10/10/11/11/11/12/12 cm) in stockinette stitch in turned rows, ending with a WS row. Break the working yarn.

Join new working yarn at the left edge of the Front and work a complete RS row. In this RS row, knit the previously doubled stitches together again and join work into the round again.

RS Row: K20/20/22/22/22/24/24 (Left Front), ssk, k2tog, k127/133/139/145/161/173/193 (Side/Back), ssk, k2tog, k20/20/22/22/22/24/24 (Right Front). You now have again 171/177/187/193/209/225/245 sts on the needles.

Work, beginning with a WS row, an additional 0.75 in (2 cm) in stockinette stitch in turned rows, ending this part with a WS row. The piece should now have reached a length of approximately 19/19/20/20/20.75/21.25/21.25 in (48/48/51/51/53/54/54 cm). Change to US 6 (4.0 mm) needles and work 2 in (5 cm) in 1 × 1 ribbing.

Now change to contrasting (Sleeve) color and work 2 rows (1 RS row and 1 WS row) in contrasting color in 1 × 1 ribbing, working all sts as they appear (knitting the knits and purling the purls). Change to main color again and work 2 rows in main color (1 RS row and 1 WS row) in 1 × 1 ribbing, working all sts as they appear (knitting the knits and purling the purls). Bind off all sts using the Italian bind-off method (page 29).

Sleeves
The Sleeves are worked in a contrasting color.
Pick up and knit a total of 76/78/82/84/88/94/102 sts around the 1st armhole at a rate of 2 sts picked up from every 3 sts. Begin picking up in the center of the underarm sts and work upward over the Shoulder and back down again to the underarm. Join to work in the round and place a marker for the BoR. Place an additional marker for the highest Shoulder point after 38/39/41/42/44/47/51 sts.

Work wrap and turn short rows (pages 14–15) to shape the Sleeve cap as follows:
Knit to Shoulder point marker, slip m, k7, turn work. P7, slip m, p7, turn work.
Following the established sequence, work 8 more turns on each side, always working to 3 sts after the previous turn; the turning stitch of the previous row is always the 1st stitch of the 3 sts. Short rows for Sleeve cap shaping have now been completed.

Work in stockinette stitch in the round with Sleeve tapering decreases at the underside of the Sleeve in every 10th/10th/10th/10th/8th/8th/8th rnd, 8/8/8/8/10/10/12 times in all.
Work **decrease rounds** as follows: K1, k2tog, k to last 3 sts, ssk, k1.
After having completed 8/8/8/8/10/10/12 decreases, a total of 80/80/80/80/80/80/96 rounds have been worked. The Sleeve has now reached a length of 12.25/12.25/12.25/12.25/12.25/12.25/14.25 in (31/31/31/31/31/31/36 cm). There are 60/62/66/68/68/74/78 sts on the needles.
Continue to work in stockinette stitch in the round until the Sleeve measures 15.0/15.4/15.8/16.1/16.5/17.0/17.3 in (38/39/40/41/42/43/44 cm) from the underarm. At this point, the Sleeve can be lengthened or shortened according to your personal preferences.
Work 1 last decrease round; during this round, k2tog a total of 10/10/12/12/10/14/16 times, evenly spaced throughout the round.
Change to US 6 (4.0 mm) needles and work 2 in (5 cm) in 1 × 1 ribbing.
Now change to main (Body) color and work 2 rounds in 1 × 1 ribbing, working all sts as they appear.
Change back to Sleeve color and work 2 rows in 1 × 1 ribbing, working all sts as they appear.
Bind off all sts using the Italian bind-off method (page 29).
Work the 2nd Sleeve the same way.

Button Band
Using US 6 (4.0 mm) needles, pick up and knit stitches from the front edge at a rate of 8 sts picked up from every 9 sts. At the right edge of the Front, begin at the bottom and work toward the top in the direction of the neckline. At the left edge, begin at the neckline opening and work down to the bottom edge. Pick up and knit a total of 123/123/131/131/135/135/137/137 sts along the 1st edge. If your stitch count is different, make sure to pick up an odd number of stitches.
Row 1 (WS): Selv st, [p1, k1] to last 2 sts, p1, selv st.
Please note: Selvedge stitches located in the Button Band are worked as described on page 68.
Work 1.25 in (3.5 cm) in 1 × 1 ribbing, working all sts as they appear (knitting the knits and purling the

purls). Purl 1 round. Then, work another 1.25 in (3.5 cm) in 1 × 1 ribbing as before. Bind off all sts using the Italian bind-off method (page 29).

Work the 2nd Front Band the same way as the 1st.

Pocket Plackets

Pocket plackets in 1 × 1 ribbing will now be knitted onto the existing piece.

Using US 6 (4.0 mm) needles and main (Body) color, pick up and knit a total of 25/25/27/27/27/31/31 sts from the side of the 1st Pocket Opening facing the Front edge.

Row 1 (WS): Selv st, [p1, k1] to last 2 sts, p1, selv st.
Please note: Selvedge stitches located in the Pocket Opening are worked as described on page 68.

Work 1 in (2.5 cm) in 1 × 1 ribbing, working all sts as they appear (knitting the knits and purling the purls). Change to contrasting (Sleeve) color and work 2 rows (1 RS row and 1 WS row) in 1 × 1 ribbing, working all sts as they appear. Change to main color again and work 2 rows (1 RS row and 1 WS row) in 1 × 1 ribbing, working all sts as they appear. Bind off all sts using the Italian bind-off method (page 29).

Work the 2nd Pocket Placket on the other Front exactly mirror-inverted to the 1st.

Pocket Lining

Using DPN set in size US 7 (4.5 mm) and contrasting (Sleeve) color, pick up and knit a total of 50/50/54/54/54/62/62 sts from the 1st Pocket Opening. Begin at the bottom corner of the opening and work upward along 1 side, then back downward along the other side. Join into the round and place a marker to indicate the BoR.

Work 4.25 in (11 cm) in stockinette stitch in the round. Turn the Pocket Lining inside out so that the wrong side of the fabric faces you. Now place 25/25/27/27/27/31/31 sts for each side on separate needles, hold them parallel, and bind off the sts from both needles together using the 3-needle-bind-off method (page 30). Work the 2nd Pocket Lining the same way as the 1st.

Collar

Fold both Button Bands to the inside and sew them with small, neat stitches to the pick-up edge. They are now double layered. Using US 6 (4.0 mm) needles, 16 in (40 cm) long, pick up a total of 93/95/97/99/103/107/111 sts along the neckline edge and along the top edges of the double-layered Button Bands at a rate of 3 sts picked up from every 4 sts. Begin at the Button Band on the Right Front and work over the Back neckline to the Button Band on the Left Front. If your stitch count is different, make sure to pick up an odd number of stitches.

Row 1 (WS): Selv st, [p1, k1] to last 2 sts, k1, selv st.

Now begin working wrap and turn short rows (pages 14–15) at the Collar:

RS Row: Work in 1 × 1 ribbing pattern as the sts appear to last 2 sts, turn work.
WS Row: Work in 1 × 1 ribbing pattern as the sts appear to last 2 sts, turn work.

Work 5 more turns for each side, always turning 2 sts before the last turning point.

Work a RS row over all remaining stitches of the (short) row.

In the next WS row, knit all stitches, which creates the fold line row.

Begin working short rows again:

RS Row: Work in 1 × 1 ribbing to last 12 sts, turn work.
WS Row: Work in 1 × 1 ribbing to last 12 sts, turn work.

Work 5 more turns for each side, always turning 2 sts past the last turning point.

Work 1 RS and 1 WS row over all stitches. Bind off all sts using the Italian bind-off method (page 29).

Finishing

Weave in all ends and attach the Pocket Plackets with 1 stitch each at the top and bottom to the Body of the cardigan. Turn the Collar over and sew it on along the pick-up edge with small, neat stitches. After this, sew the snap buttons evenly spaced onto the Button Band. For a woman's cardigan, the Button Band on the Right Front of the garment is on top, and the band on the Left Front underneath, since the Right Front is closed over the Left Front. For a man's cardigan, the Button Band on the Left Front of the garment is on top, and the band on the Right Front underneath, since the Left Front is closed over the Right Front.

Soak the cardigan in lukewarm water with a mild wool detergent. To block, spread it out flat on a horizontal surface, pin it to shape, and let it dry.

Sam

A cozy cottage sweater with comfortable turtleneck and beautiful textured cable on the front, Sam is ideal for pleasant hours by the fireplace—or perhaps your next ski trip?

MATERIALS
· Rauwerk Original; DK weight; 100% Bavarian merino wool; 241 yds (220 m) per 3.5 oz (100 g) skein; in Quarz: 5/6/7/9 skeins
  Total yardage required: 1,094/1,312/1,531/ 1,968.5 yds (1,000/1,200/1,400/1,800 m)
· Circular knitting needles in size US 8 (5.0 mm), 16 in (40 cm), 24 in (60 cm), 32 in (80 cm), and 40/ 48 in (100/120 cm) long
· Circular knitting needles in size US 7 (4.5 mm), 16 in (40 cm) and 40 in (100 cm) long
· DPN sets in size US 8 (5.0 mm) and US 7 (4.5 mm)
· Tapestry needle for weaving in ends
· Stitch markers

SIZES
1/3/5/7
Incorporated positive ease: 8–13.75 in (20–35 cm)
Chest circumference: 42/48.75/54.25/59.75 in (107/ 124/138/152 cm)
Upper arm circumference: 14.5/16.5/17.75/19.25 in (37/42/45/49 cm)
Length: 20.5/22.75/23.5/23.5 in (52/58/60/60 cm)
Our model wears size 3 (Women's M/L / Men's S/M)

GAUGE
17 sts and 26 rows = 4 × 4 in (10 × 10 cm) in stockinette stitch on US 8 (5.0 mm) needles (after washing and blocking)

STITCH PATTERNS
Cable Pattern Mix for the Front
Please note that each size has its own knitting chart, showing the entire neckline and the beginning of the Front. Only RS rows are shown in the chart. In WS rows, work all sts as they appear (knitting the knits and purling the purls). Take note that working through the back loop should be carried over to the WS rows, too: stitches knitted through the back loop in RS rows will be purled through the back loop in the following WS row.

Follow the knitting chart for your size row by row to set up the stitch pattern on the Front correctly and to shape the neckline. Once the full stitch pattern has been set up for the Front, it will be easy to follow the pattern repeat.

1 × 1 ribbing for Turtleneck Collar, Sleeve cuffs, and bottom edge
Alternate knit 1, purl 1.

Selvedge stitches
All selvedge stitches in all rows are knitted.

CONSTRUCTION NOTES
Work starts at the top of the Back in stockinette stitch, first working Shoulder increases, followed by armhole increases.

Then the Right and Left Front are worked according to the chart, and the neckline is formed. After having worked a section in the stitch pattern, armhole increases are worked before the Body is joined into the round and worked in the stitch pattern (on the Front) and in stockinette stitch (on the Back). Sleeve stitches are picked up around the armhole, the Sleeve cap is shaped, then the Sleeves are completed in stockinette stitch. Finally, the Turtleneck Collar is worked in 1 × 1 ribbing onto the neckline edge.

Turtleneck Sweater with Cable Panels on the Front

LOOSE FIT/
OVERSIZED

LET'S START

Upper Back

Using US 8 (5.0 mm) needles, 24 in (60 cm) long, and a stretchy cast-on method, cast on 32/36/40/44 sts.
Row 1 is a WS row. Place 2 markers as follows: Selv st, p2, place m, purl to last 3 sts, place m, p2, selv st. From here on, increases will be worked in every row (RS and WS rows) immediately adjacent to the markers. Work the following 2 rows 13/15/17/19 times:
RS Row: Selv st, k2, slip m, M1L from the bar between sts, knit to m, M1R from the bar between sts, slip m, k2, selv st.
WS Row: Selv st, p2, slip m, M1L from the bar between sts, purl to m, M1R from the bar between sts, slip m, p2, selv st.
You have now increased 26/30/34/36 sts on each side. There are 84/96/108/120 sts on the needles.
Work 4/4/4/4.25 in (10/10/10/11 cm) in stockinette stitch in turned rows, ending this part with a WS row. Now armhole increases will be worked in every other row, always in a RS row.
Work the following 2 rows 5/7/7/7 times:
RS Row: Selv st, k2, slip m, M1L from the bar between sts, knit to m, M1R from the bar between sts, slip m, k2, selv st.
WS Row: Work all sts as they appear (knitting the knits and purling the purls), slipping all markers when you encounter them.

There are 94/110/122/134 sts on the needles. Break the working yarn and transfer these stitches to a piece of waste yarn, an extra needle, or a spare cord for holding.

Upper Left Front

For the Left Front, pick up and knit 26/31/37/43 sts. Begin picking up at the neckline opening and pick up 1 st from each selvedge stitch of the Back. Finish picking up at the Shoulder point of the armhole. Row 1 is a RS row.
Work all stitches of Rows 1–26/1–30/1–30/1–30 according to the chart for your size.

Please note: All neckline increases are worked directly adjacent to the selv st as M1L from the bar between stitches and are either knitted or purled as shown in the chart.

Upper Right Front

For the Right Front, pick up and knit 26/31/37/43 sts. Begin picking up at the Shoulder point of the armhole and pick up 1 st from each selvedge stitch of the Back. Finish picking up at the neckline opening. Row 1 is a RS row.
Work all stitches of Rows 1–26/1–30/1–30/1–30 according to the chart for your size.

Please note: All neckline increases are worked directly adjacent to the selv st as M1R from the bar between stitches and are either knitted or purled as shown in the chart.

Now, the Upper Left Front and the Upper Right Front will be joined.
For this, work a RS row over all stitches of the Right Front as shown in the chart (= Row 27/31/31/31), extend the row by casting on 20/22/22/22 new sts, and work all sts of the Left Front as shown in the chart (= Row 27/31/31/31). You have now joined both Fronts. There are 84/98/110/122 sts on the needles. Work all sections of the stitch pattern according to the pattern repeat shown in the chart until the Front measures approximately 8/8.75/9.5/10.5 in (20/22/24/27 cm) from the cast-on edge at the Shoulder. Now it's time to begin the armhole increases. Work the armhole increases in every other row, always in a RS row, 5/7/7/7 times in all.
On the right armhole, increases are worked directly adjacent to the selv st as M1L from the bar between

sts and are worked keeping in the 2 × 2 ribbing pattern coming from the Shoulder.

On the left armhole, increases are worked around the armhole directly adjacent to the selv st as M1R from the bar between sts and are likewise worked keeping in the 2 × 2 ribbing pattern coming from the Shoulder. You should now have a total of 94/112/124/136 sts on the needles.

Body

Front and Back are now joined to form the Body: work a RS row over all sts of the Front according to the pattern repeat, CO 2 new underarm sts, knit over all sts of the Back, CO 2 new underarm sts, place a marker to indicate the BoR.

The newly cast-on underarm stitches will be knitted. There are 182/212/236/260 sts on the needles.

Work in the round, in Textured Pattern on the Front and in stockinette stitch on the Back, until the sweater measures 18/20.5/21.25/22 in (46/52/54/56 cm) from the Shoulder. The top will look especially eye-pleasing if you end after half a heightwise pattern repeat of the diamond motif. Change to US 7 (4.5 mm) needles and work 2.25 in (6 cm) in 1 × 1 ribbing.

Bind off all sts using the Italian bind-off method (page 29).

Sleeves

Pick up and knit a total of 62/74/78/86 sts around the 1st armhole at a rate of 1 st picked up from every 2. Begin picking up in the center of the underarm sts and work upward over the Shoulder and back down again to the underarm. Join into the round and place a marker to indicate the BoR. Place an additional marker for the Shoulder point after 31/37/39/43 sts.

Work wrap and turn short rows (pages 14–15) to shape the Sleeve cap as follows:

Knit to Shoulder point marker, slip m, k7, turn work. P7, slip m, p7, turn work.

Following the established sequence, work 6 more turns on each side, always working to 3 sts after the previous turn; the turning stitch of the previous row is always the 1st stitch of the 3 sts.

Short rows for Sleeve cap shaping have now been completed.

Work in stockinette stitch in the round with Sleeve tapering decreases at the underside of the Sleeve in every 12th/9th/9th/8th rnd, 7/10/10/11 times in all.

Work the **decrease round** as follows: K1, k2tog, k to last 3 sts, ssk, k1.

After having completed 7/10/10/11 decreases, a total of 84/90/90/88 rounds have been worked. The Sleeve has now reached a length of 12.5/13.5/13.5/13 in (32/34/34/33 cm). There are 48/54/58/64 sts on the needles. Continue to work in stockinette stitch in the round until the Sleeve measures 15/15.25/15.75/16.25/16.5/17/17.25 in (38/39/40/41/42/43/44 cm) from the underarm. At this point, the Sleeve can be lengthened or shortened according to your personal preferences. Change to US 7 (4.5 mm) needles and work 2.25 in (6 cm) in 1 × 1 ribbing.

Bind off all sts using the Italian bind-off method (page 29). Work the 2nd Sleeve the same way.

Turtleneck Collar

Using US 7 (4.5 mm) needles, 16 in (40 cm) long, pick up a total of 82/94/98/98 sts around the neckline edge for the Turtleneck. Begin picking up in the center of the Back. Join work into the round and place a marker to indicate the BoR. Work 7.5/8/8.25/8.75 in (19/20/21/22 cm) in 1 × 1 ribbing. Bind off all sts using the Italian bind-off method (page 29).

Finishing

Weave in all ends and soak your turtleneck sweater in lukewarm water with a mild wool detergent. Block it spread out flat on an even, horizontal surface, and let it dry.

KNITTING CHARTS

Size 1, Left Front

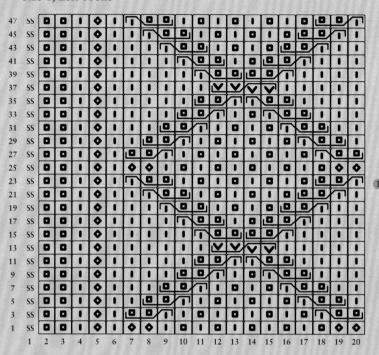

Size 1, Right Front

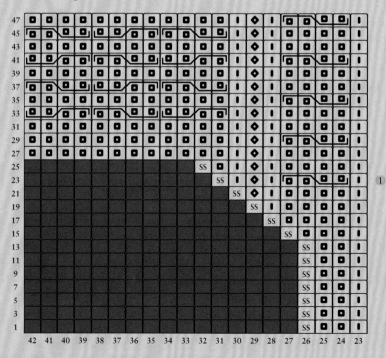

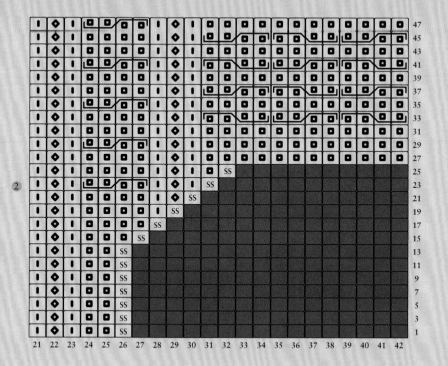

2

Knitting Symbols

$\boxed{\blacksquare}$ = knit

$\boxed{\textbf{I}}$ = purl

$\boxed{\blacklozenge}$ = RS: k-tbl, WS: p-tbl

$\boxed{\vee}\boxed{\vee}\boxed{\vee}\boxed{\vee}$ = hold 2 sts on a cable needle behind work, k2-tbl, then work the sts from the cable needle as k-tbl

$\boxed{\blacksquare}\boxed{\blacksquare}\boxed{\textbf{I}}$ = hold 1 st on a cable needle behind work, k2-tbl, then knit the st from the cable needle

$\boxed{\textbf{I}}\boxed{\blacksquare}\boxed{\blacksquare}$ = hold 2 sts on a cable needle in front of work, p1, then work the sts from the cable needle as k-tbl

$\boxed{\blacksquare}\boxed{\blacksquare}\boxed{\blacksquare}\boxed{\blacksquare}$ = hold 2 sts on a cable needle behind work, k2, then knit the sts from the cable needle

$\boxed{\blacksquare}\boxed{\blacksquare}\boxed{\blacksquare}\boxed{\blacksquare}$ = hold 2 sts on a cable needle in front of work, k2, then knit the sts from the cable needle

SS = selvedge stitch(es)

$\blacksquare$ = no stitch, for a better overview only

79

Size 3, Left Front

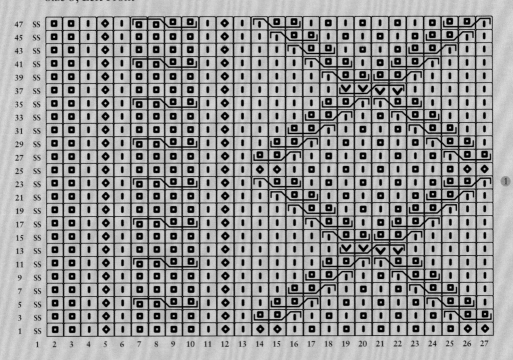

Size 3, Right Front

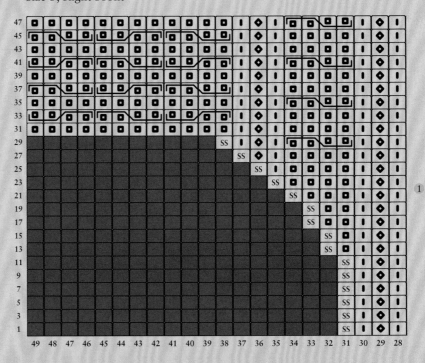

80

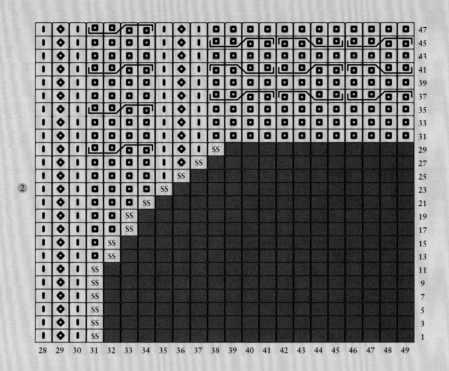

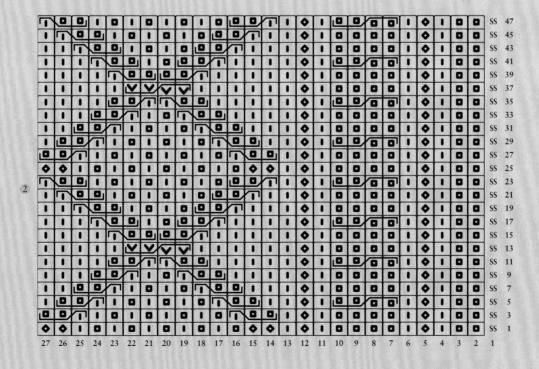

Size 5, Left Front

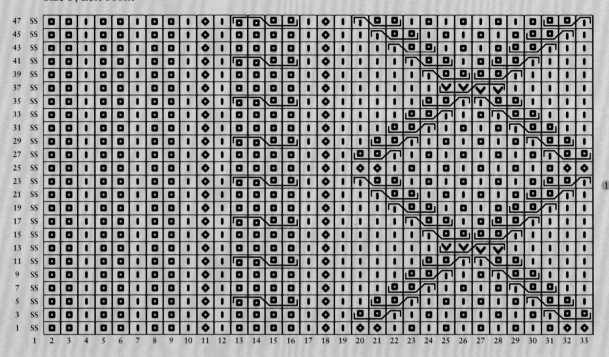

Size 5, Right Front

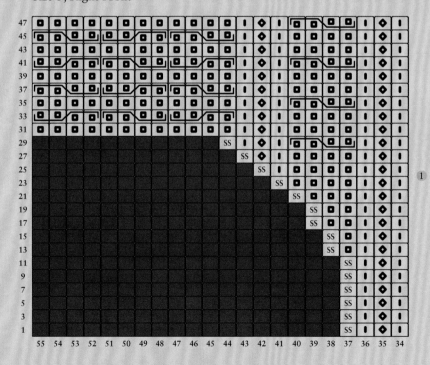

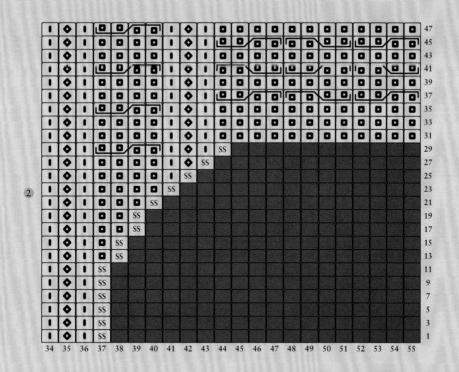

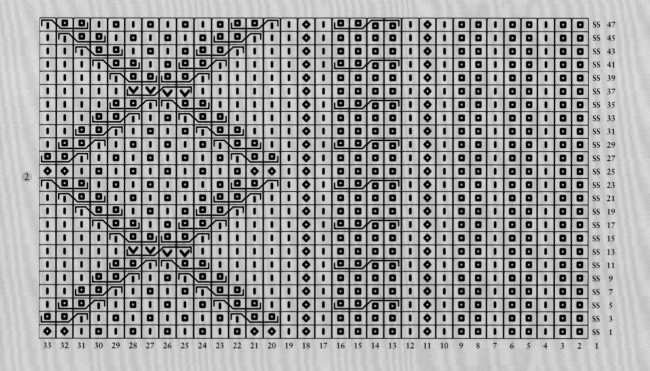

Size 7, Left Front

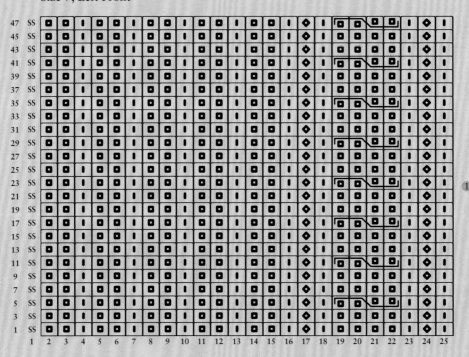

Size 7, Right Front

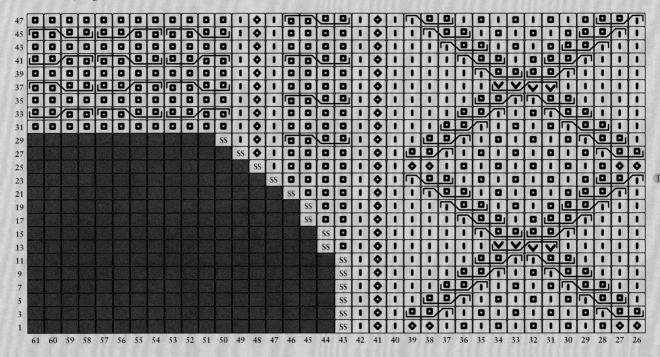

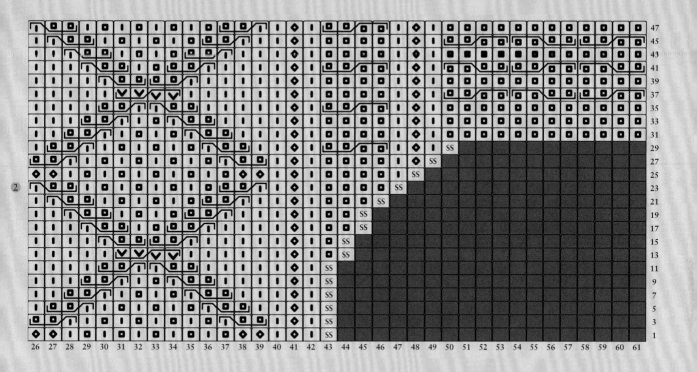

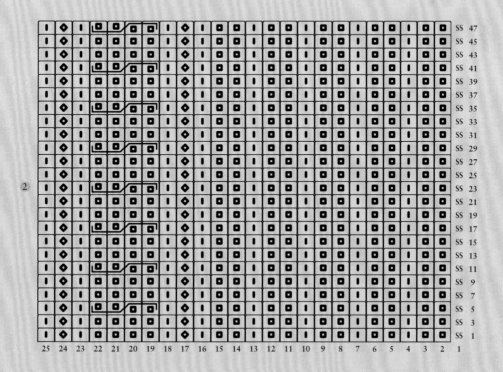

85

Toni

The sleek raglan sweater (pictured far right on page 87) in a dark color impresses with an easy textured pattern on the front and back. Depending on the yarn used, Toni can be a winter or spring/fall garment.

MATERIALS
· 1 strand Lang Yarns Merino +; worsted weight; 100% extra fine merino wool; 98.5 yds (90 m) per 1.75 oz (50 g) skein; in 152.0296 Dark Beige Heathered: 10/11/12/14/16/18/20 skeins
held together with
1 strand Lang Yarns Cashmere Lace; sport weight; 100% cashmere; 180 yds (165 m) per 0.9 oz (25 g); in 883.0067 Light Brown Heathered: 6/6/7/8/9/10/11 skeins
Total yardage required: 930/1,038/1,148/1,367/1,531/1,750/1,968.5 yds (850/950/1,050/1,250/1,400/1,600/1,800 m)
Modifying the length of the garment will change the total yarn requirements accordingly.
· Circular knitting needles in size US 9 (5.5 mm), 16 in (40 cm), 24 in (60 cm), 32 in (80 cm), and 40/48 in (100/120 cm) long
· Circular knitting needles in size US 8 (5.0 mm), 16 in (40 cm) and 32/40 in (80/100 cm) long
· DPN sets in size US 8 (5.0 mm) and US 9 (5.5 mm)
· Tapestry needle for weaving in ends
· Stitch markers

SIZES
1/2/3/4/5/6/7
Incorporated positive ease: 4–7 in (10–18 cm)
Chest circumference: 37.75/39.75/43/45/49.25/52.75/55.5 in (96/101/109/114/125/134/141 cm)
Upper arm circumference: 12.5/13.5/13.75/15/15.75/17.25/19 in (32/34/35/38/40/44/48 cm)
Length: 20.5/21/21.25/21.75/22/22.5/22.75 in (52/53/54/55/56/57/58 cm)
Our model wears size 5 (Women's XL / Men's L)

GAUGE
15 sts and 24 rows = 4 × 4 in (10 × 10 cm) in stockinette stitch with 1 strand of each yarn held together on US 9 (5.5 mm) needles (after washing and blocking)

STITCH PATTERNS
Textured Pattern for Front and Back in rounds
The main pattern for Front and Back has a pattern repeat of 2 sts widthwise and 8 rounds heightwise.
Rnds 1–4: *K1, p1, rep from * around.
Rnds 5–8: *P1, k1, rep from * around.

1 × 1 ribbing
Alternate knit 1, purl 1.

CONSTRUCTION NOTES
The sweater is worked seamlessly from the top down in one piece. Work starts with the double-layered neckband in 1 × 1 ribbing, which is shaped with short rows. Then the Yoke is divided into sections and worked in the round with raglan increases. The Sleeves are worked in stockinette stitch, Front and Back in a textured pattern. Then the Sleeve stitches are placed on hold, and the Body is worked in the round featuring a textured pattern, then the Sleeves are completed in stockinette stitch in the round. Sleeve cuffs and the Body's bottom edge are worked in 1 × 1 ribbing.
Work with 1 strand of each yarn held together throughout.

RELAXED FIT

LET'S START

Note: Work with 1 strand of each yarn held together throughout.

Neckband

Using circular needle in size US 8 (5.0 mm), 16 in (40 cm) long, and a stretchy cast-on method, cast on 84/84/88/80/92/84/84 sts.

Join work into the round, taking care not to twist the cast-on row. Place a marker to indicate the BoR. The BoR is located in the center Back.

Work 1 round in 1 × 1 ribbing. Then work wrap and turn short rows (pages 14–15) as follows:

30 sts in 1 × 1 ribbing, working all sts as they appear (knitting the knits and purling the purls); turn work.

60 sts in 1 × 1 ribbing, working all sts as they appear; turn work.

54 sts in 1 × 1 ribbing, working all sts as they appear; turn work.

48 sts in 1 × 1 ribbing, working all sts as they appear; turn work.

42 sts in 1 × 1 ribbing, working all sts as they appear; turn work.

36 sts in 1 × 1 ribbing, working all sts as they appear; turn work.

Work all sts in 1 × 1 ribbing, as they appear, to BoR marker.

Work 9 rounds in 1 × 1 ribbing, working all sts as they appear.

Purl 1 round (fold line).

Work 9 rounds in 1 × 1 ribbing, working all sts as they appear.

18 sts in 1 × 1 ribbing, working all sts as they appear; turn work.

36 sts in 1 × 1 ribbing, working all sts as they appear; turn work.

42 sts in 1 × 1 ribbing, working all sts as they appear; turn work.

45 sts in 1 × 1 ribbing, working all sts as they appear; turn work.

54 sts in 1 × 1 ribbing, working all sts as they appear; turn work.

60 sts in 1 × 1 ribbing, working all sts as they appear; turn work.

Work all sts in 1 × 1 ribbing, working all sts as they appear, to BoR marker. Remove the BoR marker.

Yoke

Work 1 last round in 1 × 1 ribbing, while dividing the Yoke into sections using markers and moving the BoR as follows:

Work 10/10/12/10/12/12/12 sts in 1 × 1 ribbing (Back), place m, 7 sts in 1 × 1 ribbing (raglan sts), place marker (this will be the new BoR), work 9/9/7/7/7/5/3 sts in 1 × 1 ribbing (Sleeve), place m, work 7 sts in 1 × 1 ribbing (raglan sts), place m, work 19/19/23/19/25/23/25 sts in 1 × 1 ribbing (Front), place m, 7 sts in 1 × 1 ribbing (raglan sts), place m, 9/9/7/7/7/5/3 sts in 1 × 1 ribbing (Sleeve), place m, 7 sts in 1 × 1 ribbing (raglan sts), place m, 19/19/23/19/25/23/25 sts in 1 × 1 ribbing, slip m, 7 sts in 1 × 1 ribbing (raglan sts). You have now reached the new BoR. Change to US 9 (5.5 mm) needles.

From here on, raglan increases will be worked in every other round, always before (to the right of) and after (to the left of) the raglan stitches.

Sleeve stitches will be knitted from now on; for this reason, the increased stitches on the Sleeve will also always be knitted.

The stitches of the Front and the Back are from here on worked in a textured pattern; for this reason, the increased stitches on the Front and Back will be worked using the pattern repeat of the Textured Pattern.

If the 1st existing stitch after—or the last existing stitch before—the increase is a knit stitch, the increased stitch will be purled.

If the 1st existing stitch after—or the last existing stitch before—the increase is a purl stitch, the increased stitch will be knitted.

Watch out when the stitch pattern changes within the pattern repeat (Rnds 1 and 5)! Here special attention is required, since the way the 1st existing stitch after—or the last existing stitch before—the increase must be worked will change!

The 7 raglan stitches at each raglan spot are worked as before in 1 × 1 ribbing, working all sts as they appear.

Work the following 2 rounds 16/20/20/24/24/28/32 times:

Rnd 1: M1L from the bar between sts, knit to m, M1R from the bar between sts, slip m, work the 7 raglan sts in 1 × 1 ribbing as the sts appear, slip m, M1L from the bar between sts, work the Textured Pattern to marker, M1R from the bar between sts, slip m, work the 7 raglan sts as they appear, slip m, M1L from the bar between sts, knit to m, M1R from the bar between sts, slip m, work the 7 raglan sts as they appear, slip m, M1L from the bar between sts, work the Textured Pattern to marker, M1R from the bar between sts, slip m, work the 7 raglan sts as they appear, to BoR marker. **Rnd 2:** Work all raglan sts and all Sleeve sts as they appear and all sts of the Front and Back in the Textured Pattern.

Make sure to remember that in every 4th rnd the stitch pattern in the Textured Pattern changes!

There are 212/244/248/272/284/308/340 sts on the needles: 7 raglan sts each, 41/49/47/55/55/61/67 sts for each Sleeve, and 51/59/63/67/73/79/89 sts each for Front and Back. A total of 32/40/40/48/48/56/64 rounds have been worked, during which the pattern repeat of the Textured Pattern has been worked 4/5/5/6/6/7/8 times in all.

Body

Now the Sleeve stitches will be placed on hold. Raglan stitches are reallocated to the Body and will be from here on incorporated into the pattern repeat of the Textured Pattern on the Front and Back, as will the newly cast-on underarm stitches, so that all of the Body will be worked in Textured Pattern.

Transfer the 1st 41/49/47/55/55/61/67 sts to a stitch holder, spare cord, or piece of waste yarn for holding, CO 7/3/5/5/7/7/7 new underarm stitches, remove m, work 7 sts according to the pattern repeat for the Textured Pattern (to match the stitch pattern on the Front and Back), remove m, work 51/59/63/67/73/79/89 sts according to the pattern repeat for the Textured Pattern, remove m, work 7 sts according to the pattern repeat for the Textured Pattern (to match the stitch pattern on the Front and Back), remove m, transfer 41/49/47/55/55/61/67 sts to a stitch holder, spare cord, or piece of waste yarn for holding, CO 7/3/5/5/7/7/7 new underarm stitches, remove m, work 7 sts according to the pattern repeat for the Textured Pattern (to match the stitch pattern on the Front and Back), remove m, work 51/59/63/67/73/79/89 sts according to the pattern repeat for the Textured Pattern, remove m, work 7 sts according to the pattern repeat for the Textured Pattern (to match the stitch pattern on the Front and Back). You have now again reached the marker for the BoR. There are 144/152/164/172/188/200/220 sts on the needles. Make sure to change the stitch pattern in this 1st row of the Body and to begin the pattern repeat anew.

Work in Textured Pattern in the round until the Body measures approximately 18/18.5/19/19.25/19.75/20/20.5 in (46/47/48/49/50/51/52 cm). End this part with either a Round 4 or a Round 8 of the pattern repeat. Change to US 8 (5.0 mm) needles and work 2.25 in (6 cm) in 1 × 1 ribbing, during the 1st round of ribbing always working a knit stitch where there had been a purl stitch in the Body pattern, and vice versa and, in subsequent rounds, working all sts as they appear (knitting the knits and purling the purls). Bind off all sts using the Italian bind-off method (page 29).

Sleeves

Place the 41/49/47/55/61/67 previously held sts of the 1st Sleeve onto a circular needle in size US 9 (5.5 mm), 16 in (40 cm) long, and knit 7/3/5/3/5/5/5 sts into the newly cast-on Body sts (= 48/52/52/58/60/66/72 sts). After 3 sts of the newly cast-on sts, place a marker for the BoR.

Now work in stockinette stitch in the round, at the same time working Sleeve tapering decreases at the underside of the Sleeve in every 14th/12th/12th/9th/9th/8th/8th rnd, a total of 5/6/6/8/8/10/12 times.

Work **Sleeve tapering decrease round** as follows: K1, ssk, k to last 3 sts, k2tog, k1.

After having completed 5/6/6/8/8/10/12 decreases, a total of 70/72/72/72/72/80/72 rounds have been worked. The Sleeve has now reached a length of 11.5/11.75/11.75/11.75/11.75/11.75/13/11.75 in (29/30/30/30/30/30/33/30 cm). There are 38/40/40/42/44/46/48 sts on the needles.

Continue to work in stockinette stitch in the round until the Sleeve measures 15/15/15.25/15.25/15.75/15.75/16.25 in (38/38/39/39/40/40/41 cm) from armhole. At this point, the Sleeve can be lengthened or shortened according to your personal preferences.

Change to US 8 (5.0 mm) needles and work 2.25 in (6 cm) in 1 × 1 ribbing. Bind off all sts using the Italian bind-off method (page 29).

Work the 2nd Sleeve the same way.

Finishing

Weave in all ends, fold the neckband to the inside, and sew it on using small, neat stitches. Soak the sweater in lukewarm water with a mild wool detergent. Block it spread out flat on an even, horizontal surface, and let it dry.

Luca

When warm comfort is needed, Luca is in demand! This turtleneck sweater is an intermediate-level pattern that works up quickly and easily. It is the perfect feel-good companion for every occasion due to the wonderfully soft quality of the yarn. Worked to a tunic length, it can be combined with leggings and boots in a beautifully feminine way.

MATERIALS
· *For the short sweater:* Pascuali Cashmere Worsted; worsted weight; 100% organic cashmere wool; 61 yds (56 m) per 0.9 oz (25 g); in 04 Graphite: 16/17/19/22/25/27/30 skeins
Total yardage required: 930/1,038/1,148/1,312/1,476/1,640/1,804.5 yds (850/950/1,050/1,200/1,350/1,500/1,650 m)
· *For the tunic-length sweater:*
1 strand Rauwerk Original; DK weight; 100% Bavarian merino wool; 241 yds (220 m) per 3.5 oz (100 g) skein; in Sand: 6/6/7/8/9/9/10 skeins
held together with
1 strand Lang Yarns Lace; sport weight; 58% superkid mohair, 42% silk, 339 yds (310 m) per 0.9 oz (25 g); in 992.0039: 4/5/5/6/6/7/7 skeins
Total yardage required: 1,312/1,422/1,586/1,750/1,968.5/2,133/2,297 yds (1,200/1,300/1,450/1,600/1,800/1,950/2,100 m)
Modifying the length of the garment will change the total yarn requirements accordingly.
· Circular knitting needles in size US 8 (5.0 mm), 24 in (60 cm), 32 in (80 cm), and 40/48 in (100/120 cm) long
· Circular knitting needle in size US 7 (4.5 mm), 16 in (40 cm) long
· Circular knitting needle in size US 6 (4.0 mm), 32 in (80 cm) long
· DPN sets in sizes US 6 (4.0 mm) and US 8 (5.0 mm)
· Tapestry needle for weaving in ends
· Stitch markers

SIZES
1/2/3/4/5/6/7
Incorporated positive ease: 4–7 in (10–18 cm)
Chest circumference: 37/40.5/43/46/48/52/55.5 in (94/103/109/117/122/132/141 cm)
Upper arm circumference: 12.5/14.5/14.5/16.5/16.5/18.5/20 in (32/37/37/42/42/47/51 cm)

Length of short sweater (see page 93 for Tunic Length Modifications): 21.25/21.75/22/22.5/22.75/23.2/23.5 in (54/55/56/57/58/59/60 cm)
Short sweater: Our model wears size 4 (Women's M / Men's S)
Tunic-length sweater: Our model wears size 2 (Women's S / Men's XS)

GAUGE
17 sts × 25 rows = 4 × 4 in (10 × 10 cm) in stockinette stitch (with 1 strand of yarn as indicated for the short sweater and 2 strands held together for the tunic-length sweater) on US 8 (5.0 mm) needles after washing and blocking

STITCH PATTERNS
2 × 2 ribbing for Turtleneck Collar and Yoke
Alternate knit 2, purl 2.

1 × 1 ribbing for Sleeve cuffs and bottom edge ribbing
Alternate knit 1, purl 1.

CONSTRUCTION NOTES
Work starts at the Turtleneck, which is worked on a short circular needle in 2 × 2 ribbing in the round. After work has been divided into sections for raglan shaping, short rows are worked before raglan increases are worked in 2 × 2 ribbing in the round.
After Sleeve stitches have been placed on hold, the Body is finished in the round—first in 2 × 2 ribbing, then in stockinette stitch. The bottom edge of the Body is worked in 1 × 1 ribbing.
Sleeves are finished last, matching to the Body on a short circular needle in the round—first in 2 × 2 ribbing, then in stockinette stitch in the round. The Sleeve cuffs, too, are worked in 1 × 1 ribbing.

RELAXED FIT

LET'S START

Turtleneck Collar

Using circular needle in size US 7 (4.5 mm), 16 in (40 cm) long, and stretchy cast-on method, cast on 88/88/96/96/104/104/104 sts.

Join work into the round, taking care not to twist the cast-on row. Place a marker to indicate the BoR. The BoR is located in the center Back.

Work 7.5/7.5/8/8/8.25/8.25/8.75 in (19/19/20/20/21/21/22 cm) in 2 × 2 ribbing.

Dividing the Yoke and Working Short Rows

Work a **setup round** in 2 × 2 ribbing, working all sts as they appear, placing 8 markers for raglan increases as follows:

Work 12/12/16/16/16/16/16 sts in 2 × 2 ribbing (Back), place m, work 6 sts in 2 × 2 ribbing (raglan sts), place m, work 10/10/10/10/10/10/10 sts in 2 × 2 ribbing (Sleeve), place m, work 6 sts in 2 × 2 ribbing (raglan sts), place m, work 22/22/26/26/30/30/30 sts in 2 × 2 ribbing (Front), place m, work 6 sts in 2 × 2 ribbing (raglan sts), place m, work 10/10/10/10/10/10/10 sts in 2 × 2 ribbing (Sleeve), place m, work 6 sts in 2 × 2 ribbing (raglan sts), place m, work 10/10/10/10/14/14/14 sts in 2 × 2 ribbing (Back). You have again reached the BoR in the center Back.

Now neckline shaping with wrap and turn short rows (pages 14–15) begins, and at the same time begin raglan increases. Raglan increases are worked to the right of (before) and to the left of (after) the raglan sts, keeping the pattern of the 2 × 2 ribbing intact and, depending on the position within the stitch pattern, are either knitted or purled in the following round. Change to US 8 (5.0 mm) needles.

Row 1 (RS): Work all sts as they appear (knitting the knits and purling the purls) to marker (Back), M1R from the bar between sts, slip m, work sts as they appear to marker (raglan sts), slip m, M1L from the bar between sts, work sts to marker (Sleeve) as they appear, M1R from the bar between sts, slip m, work sts as they appear to marker (raglan sts), slip m, M1L from the bar between sts, work 1 st as it appears, turn work.

Row 2 (WS): Work all sts as they appear to BoR marker, slipping all markers when you encounter them, slip BoR marker, work sts to marker (Back) as they appear, M1R from the bar between sts, slip m, work sts as they appear to marker (raglan sts), slip m, M1L from the bar between sts, work sts to marker (Sleeve) as they appear, M1R from the bar between sts, slip m, work sts as they appear to marker (raglan sts), slip m, M1L from the bar between sts, work 1 st as it appears, turn work.

Row 3 (RS): Work all sts as they appear to BoR marker, slipping all markers when you encounter them.

You have now completed the 1st raglan increase for each increase spot as well as worked the 1st turn for each side (= 96/96/104/104/112/112/112 sts).

Work the 3 described rows another 2 times, always working 2/2/3/3/3/3/3 sts past the previous turn. The turning stitch is always the 1st of the 2/2/3/3/3/3/3 sts. You have now worked 3 raglan increases and 3 turns for each side. All short rows have been completed (= 112/112/120/120/128/128/128 sts).

Yoke

From here on, work in 2 × 2 ribbing in the round with raglan increases until you have worked a total of 20/24/24/28/28/32/36 increases for each increase spot.

This means to work the following 2 rounds a total of 17/21/21/25/25/29/33 times:

Rnd 1: Work sts as they appear (knitting the knits and purling the purls) to marker (Back), M1R from the bar between sts, slip m, work sts as they appear to marker (raglan sts), slip m, M1L from the bar between sts, work sts to marker (Sleeve) as they appear, M1R from the bar between sts, slip m, work sts as they appear to marker (raglan sts), slip m, M1L from the bar between sts, work sts as they appear to marker (Front), M1R from the bar between sts, slip m, work sts as they appear to marker (raglan sts), slip m, M1L from the bar between sts, work sts to marker (Sleeve) as they appear, M1R from the bar between sts, slip m, work sts as they appear to marker (raglan sts), slip m, M1L from the bar between sts, work all sts as they appear to BoR marker, slip marker.

Rnd 2: Work all sts as they appear, slipping all markers when you encounter them.

You have now worked a total of 20/24/24/28/28/32/36 raglan increases. There are 248/280/288/320/328/360/392 sts on the needles: 6 raglan sts each, 62/70/74/82/86/94/102 sts each for Front and Back, and 50/58/58/66/66/74/82 sts each for each Sleeve. The Yoke has now been completed.

Body

Now Sleeve stitches are placed on hold, and raglan stitches are reallocated to the Body: Work sts as they appear (knitting the knits and purling the purls) to marker, remove m, work sts as they appear to marker, remove m, place the following 50/58/58/66/66/74/82 sts on hold, CO 6 new underarm sts, placing a marker after the 1st 4 of these 6 sts (this marker will be the new BoR), remove m, work sts as they appear to marker, remove m, work sts as they appear to marker, remove m, work sts as they appear to marker, remove m, place the following 50/58/58/66/66/74/82 sts on hold, CO 6 new underarm sts, remove m, work sts as they appear to marker, remove m, work all sts as they appear to the previous marker for the BoR, remove m, work all sts as they appear to the new marker for the BoR. There are 160/176/184/200/208/224/240 sts on the needles. Work 4/4.25/4.75/4.75/5/5/5.5 in (10/11/12/12/13/13/14 cm) in 2 × 2 ribbing in the round, incorporating the newly cast-on underarm sts into the 2 × 2 ribbing pattern. Continue in stockinette stitch in the round until a total length of 19.25/19.75/20/20.5/21/21.25/21.75 in (49/50/51/52/53/54/55 cm) from Shoulder/neckline has been reached. Change to US 6 (4.0 mm) needles and work 2 in (5 cm) in 1 × 1 ribbing. Bind off all sts using the Italian bind-off method (page 29).

Sleeves

Place the 50/58/58/66/66/74/82 previously held sts of the 1st Sleeve onto a circular needle in size US 8 (5.0 mm), 16 in (40 cm) long, and work 6 sts into the newly cast-on underarm sts at the side of the Body (= 56/64/64/72/72/80/88 sts). Place a marker for the BoR after 3 of the 6 newly cast-on Body sts. Work the newly cast-on sts as k2, p2, k2.

Then work 4/4.25/4.75/4.75/5/5/5.5 in (10/11/12/12/13/13/14 cm) in 2 × 2 ribbing, at the same time working Sleeve tapering decreases at the underside of the Sleeve in every 14th/10th/10th/8th/8th/7th/6th rnd, 6/9/8/10/10/12/16 times in all.

Work **Sleeve tapering decrease round** as follows: Work 2 sts as they appear, ssk, work sts as they appear to last 4 sts, k2tog, work 2 sts as they appear.

After having worked 4/4.25/4.75/4.75/5/5/5.5 in (10/11/12/12/13/13/14 cm) in 2 × 2 ribbing, work the remainder of the Sleeve in stockinette stitch in the round, continuing Sleeve tapering decreases as before at the established intervals.

After having completed 6/9/8/10/10/12/16 decreases, a total of 84/90/80/80/80/84/96 rounds have been worked. The Sleeve has now reached a length of 13.25/14.25/12.5/12.5/12.5/13.25/15 in (33.5/36/32/32/32/33.5/38.5 cm). There are 44/46/48/52/52/56/56 sts on the needles.

Continue to work in stockinette stitch in the round until the Sleeve measures 16.5/17/17.25/17.75/18/18.5/19 in (42/43/44/45/46/47/48 cm) from armhole. At this point, the Sleeve can be lengthened or shortened according to your personal preferences. Change to US 6 (4.0 mm) needles and work 2 in (5 cm) in 1 × 1 ribbing.

Bind off all sts using the Italian bind-off method (page 29).

Work the 2nd Sleeve the same way.

TUNIC LENGTH MODIFICATIONS

This design can be changed into a tunic-length sweater dress with just 2 little modifications: Lengthen the stockinette stitch part of the Body by approximately 6.25 in (16 cm) to a total of 25.5/26/26.25/26.75/27.25/27.5/28 in (65/66/67/68/69/70/71 cm) from the Shoulder/neckline and work the 1 × 1 bottom edge ribbing to a height of 4.75 in (12 cm) instead of 2 in (5 cm). Additionally, you can widen the raglan lines from 6 to 10 sts when dividing the Yoke by simply shifting the markers for Front and Back by 4 sts inwards in each spot. This does not affect the Sleeve stitches.

Finishing

Weave in all ends and soak the sweater in lukewarm water with a mild wool detergent. Block it spread out flat on an even, horizontal surface, and let it dry.

Sasha

This cool cardigan with side pockets impresses with the beautiful tweed structure of its yarn and the comfy stand-up collar. This contemporary style should not be missing from any wardrobe!

MATERIALS

· 1 strand Lamana Como Tweed; DK weight; 100% extra fine merino wool; 131 yds (120 m) per 0.9 oz (25 g); in 69T Fir: 14/15/19/20 skeins
held together with
1 strand Lamana Shetland; fingering weight; 100% pure new wool; 153 yds (140 m) per 0.9 oz (25 g); in 69 Fir: 12/13/16/18 skeins
Total yardage required: 1,750/1,968.5/2,406/2,625 yds (1,600/1,800/2,200/2,400 m)
· Circular knitting needles in size US 8 (5.0 mm), 2 each in 24 in (60 cm), 32 in (80 cm), and 40/48 in (100/120 cm) long
· Circular knitting needles in size US 6 (4.0 mm), 16 in (40 cm) and 48 in (120 cm) long
· DPN sets in size US 8 (5.0 mm) and US 6 (4.0 mm)
· 8 buttons, 0.8–0.9 in (21–24 mm) diameter
· Tapestry needle for weaving in ends
· Stitch markers

SIZES

1/3/5/7
Incorporated positive ease: 8–13.75 in (20–35 cm)
Chest circumference: 41.25/46/51.25/58.25 in (105/117/130/148 cm)
Upper arm circumference: 13.5/15.25/16.5/18 in (34/39/42/46 cm)
Length: 27.5/28.25/30/30.75 in (70/72/76/78 cm) measured from Shoulder to bottom edge
Our model wears size 3 (Women's M/L / Men's S/M)

GAUGE

17 sts and 26 rows = 4 × 4 in (10 × 10 cm) in stockinette stitch with 1 strand of each yarn held together on US 8 (5.0 mm) needles (after washing and blocking)

STITCH PATTERNS

Stockinette stitch in turned rows
RS Rows: Knit all stitches.
WS Rows: Purl all sts.

Stockinette stitch in the round
Knit all stitches.

Selvedge stitches
Slip the 1st stitch (purlwise) with yarn in front of work in every row, knit the last stitch in every row.

1 × 1 ribbing for bottom edge, Sleeve slits, Collar, Pocket Plackets, placket facings, and interior button and buttonhole bands facings
Alternate knit 1, purl 1.

Shoulder stitches/raglan stitches
The 3 Shoulder stitches are first set up as "purl 1, knit 1, purl 1," then always worked as the stitches appear.

CONSTRUCTION NOTES

First, the double-layered Collar is worked, then Front and Back are shaped with Shoulder increases and short rows. The Button Band is directly knitted onto the existing piece. After having completed Sleeve and raglan increases, Sleeve stitches are placed on hold and the Body continued in stockinette stitch in turned rows and finished at the bottom shirttail-style with short-row shaping. At the indicated height, Pocket Slits are incorporated. Sleeves are finished in stockinette stitch in the round. At the Sleeve cuff, the slit is worked first, followed by the cuff ribbing with buttonhole.
Plackets and lining for the set-in side Pockets are completed last.
Work with 1 strand of each yarn held together throughout.

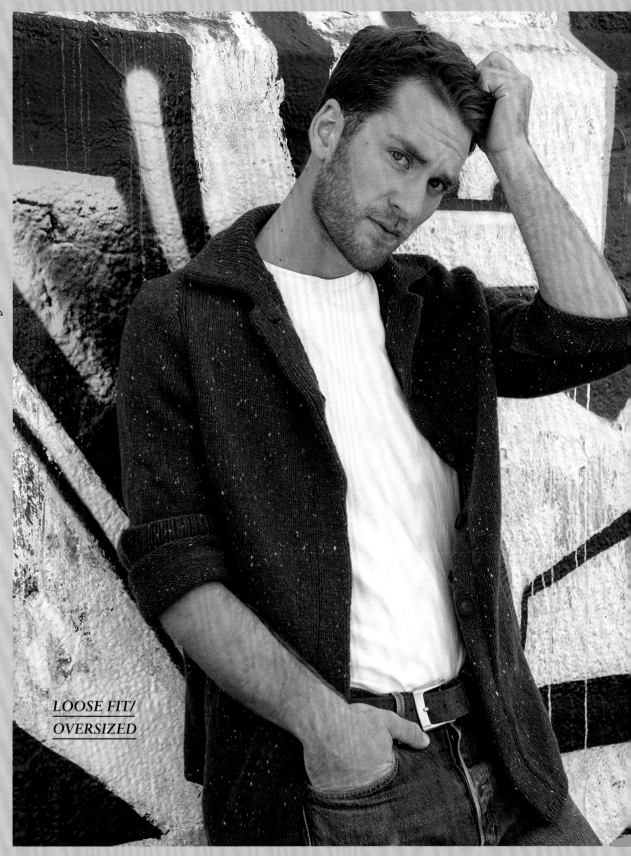

**LOOSE FIT/
OVERSIZED**

LET'S START

Note: Work with 1 strand of each yarn held together throughout, unless otherwise indicated.

Collar

Using both needle tips of a circular needle in size US 6 (4.0 mm), 48 in (120 cm) long, and the magic cast-on method (page 10), cast on 99/105/111/117 sts onto each needle tip, resulting in a total of 198/210/222/234 sts cast on.

There are 99/105/111/117 sts on the needle tip in front and 99/105/111/117 sts on the needle tip in back. Pull out the tip of the front needle to the right and begin to work the sts on the back needle in a 1 × 1 ribbing pattern until 1 st remains on the front needle, k1. Work the same RS row over all stitches of the 2nd needle. The 1 × 1 ribbing pattern for the Collar has now been set up, and you have worked 1 full round over all stitches. There are still 99/105/111/117 sts on each of the 2 needle tips facing each other.

From here on, decreases to shape the Collar will be worked at the front edges of the Collar. Work the following 4 rounds a total of 6 times:

Rnds 1–3: *Work all sts in 1 × 1 ribbing as the sts appear*.
Repeat from * to * for the stitches on the 2nd needle tip.
Rnd 4: *K1, p1, ssk, work in 1 × 1 ribbing as the sts appear to last 4 sts, k2tog, p1, k1*.
Repeat from * to * for the stitches on the 2nd needle tip.

You have now decreased 12 sts on each of the 2 needle tips. 87/93/99/105 sts remain per needle tip on the 2 needles opposite each other. Work an additional 8 rounds even without decreases in 1 × 1 ribbing, working all sts as they appear. Should there be any yarn tails in the Collar section, now is a good time to weave them in. In the next RS row, the Collar will be closed up.
Prepare the front edges for setting up the Button Band. To do this, transfer the 1st and last 7 sts from the back needle onto a single DPN in size US 8 (5.0 mm) as follows: Work the 1st 7 sts of the front needle in 1 × 1 ribbing as the sts appear. Place the 1st 7 sts of the back needle onto a DPN. Transferring 1 st at a time, slip 1 st from the back needle onto the front needle and either knit or purl them together with the current stitch as the sts appear (alternating k2tog, p2tog in

pattern). Repeat these steps until 7 sts remain on each of the front and back needles.
Work the 7 sts of the front needle in pattern as the sts appear. Then take up a single size US 8 (5.0 mm) DPN and use it to work off 6 of the 7 sts from the back needle. Knit the 7th = last stitch (selv st), then turn work.

You now have a total of 101/107/113/119 sts on the needles: 7 sts on each of the 2 DPNs and 87/93/99/105 sts on the circular needle.
In the **next (WS) row**, the knitted piece will be divided into sections using stitch markers. Additionally, a few new stitches will be cast on at the front edges. From these stitches, the 2nd half of the Button Band will be created:
On DPN: Selv st, [k1, p1] 3 times, extend the row by casting on 5 new sts.
On circular needle: CO 5 new sts, p3, k1 (visual border of the Button Band), p13/15/17/19 (Front), place m, k1, p1, k1 (Shoulder/raglan sts), p5 (Sleeve), place m, k1, p1, k1 (Shoulder/raglan sts), p31/33/35/37 (Back), place m, k1, p1, k1 (Shoulder/raglan sts), p5 (Sleeve), place m, k1, p1, k1 (Shoulder/raglan sts), p13/15/17/19, k1 (visual border of the Button Band), p3, CO 5 new sts.
On DPN: CO 5 new sts, [p1, k1] 3 times, selv st.

Including the 5 newly cast-on sts each at the front edges, you should now have a total of 121/127/133/139 sts on the needles.
The sts currently sitting on the DPNs will later become the interior facing of the Button Band. These sts will be worked in 1 × 1 ribbing, as partially already set up. Into 1 side of this interior facing, a total of 6 buttonholes will be worked in evenly spaced intervals of 4 in (10 cm) each. This creates a hidden Button Band. The newly cast-on sts will become the part of the Button Band that extends over the center of the Front. These sts will be worked as an extension of the Front and of the interior facing. At the Fronts, a single purl stitch each will be visible. This stitch is the visual border of the Button Band and is always to be worked so that it appears as a purl stitch on the right side of the knitted fabric.

Now, begin to work the Shoulder increases in turned rows, in every row. At the same time, wrap and turn short rows (pages 14–15) to improve the fit will be worked on the Front:

Row 1 (RS): Selv st, [p1, k1] 5 times, p1, needle change, work sts as they appear (knitting the knits and purling the purls) to marker, M1R from the bar between sts, slip m, p1, k1, p1 (Shoulder/raglan sts), slip m, k5 (Sleeve), slip m, p1, k1, p1 (Shoulder/raglan sts), slip m, M1L from the bar between sts, knit to m, M1R from the bar between sts, slip m, p1, k1, p1 (Shoulder/raglan sts), slip m, k5 (Sleeve), slip m, p1, k1, p1 (Shoulder/raglan sts), slip m, M1L from the bar between sts, k3, turn work.

Row 2 (WS): Work sts as they appear (knitting the knits and purling the purls) to marker, M1R from the bar between sts, slip m, k1, p1, k1 (Shoulder/raglan sts), slip m, p5 (Sleeve), slip m, k1, p1, k1 (Shoulder/raglan sts), slip m, M1L from the bar between sts, purl to m, M1R from the bar between sts, slip m, k1, p1, k1 (Shoulder/raglan sts), slip m, p5 (Sleeve), slip m, k1, p1, k1 (Shoulder/raglan sts), slip m, M1L from the bar between sts, k3, turn work.

Row 3 (RS): Work sts as they appear (knitting the knits and purling the purls) to marker, M1R from the bar between sts, slip m, p1, k1, p1 (Shoulder/raglan sts), slip m, k5 (Sleeve), slip m, p1, k1, p1 (Shoulder/raglan sts), slip m, M1L from the bar between sts, knit to m, M1R from the bar between sts, slip m, p1, k1, p1 (Shoulder/raglan sts), slip m, k5 (Sleeve), slip m, p1, k1, p1 (Shoulder/raglan sts), slip m, M1L from the bar between sts, knit to the turning stitch of the previous row, work 3 sts as they appear, turn work. Repeat the last 2 rows another 3 times, always working 3 sts past the previous turning spot; the turning stitch of the previous row is always the 1st of the 3 sts.

Work the next WS row as follows:

WS Row: Work sts as they appear (knitting the knits and purling the purls) to marker, M1R from the bar between sts, slip m, k1, p1, k1 (Shoulder/raglan sts), slip m, p5 (Sleeve), slip m, k1, p1, k1 (Shoulder/raglan sts), slip m, M1L from the bar between sts, purl to m, M1R from the bar between sts, slip m, k1, p1, k1 (Shoulder/raglan sts), slip m, p5 (Sleeve), slip m, k1, p1, k1 (Shoulder/raglan sts), slip m, M1L from the bar between sts, work all sts as they appear (knitting the knits and purling the purls) to the end of this needle, needle change, [k1, p1] 5 times, k1, selv st.

You have now increased 10 sts for each increase spot. There are 161/167/173/179 sts on the needles: 32/34/36/38 sts for each Front, 12 sts on each DPN, 3 Shoulder/raglan sts each, 51/53/55/57 sts for the Back, and 5 sts for each Sleeve.

Work the following 2 rows:

Row 1 (RS): Selv st, [p1, k1] 5 times, p1, needle change, work sts as they appear (knitting the knits and purling the purls) to marker, M1R from the bar between sts, slip m, p1, k1, p1 (Shoulder/raglan sts), slip m, k5 (Sleeve), slip m, p1, k1, p1 (Shoulder/raglan sts), slip m, M1L from the bar between sts, knit to m, M1R from the bar between sts, slip m, p1, k1, p1 (Shoulder/raglan sts), slip m, k5 (Sleeve), slip m, p1, k1, p1 (Shoulder/raglan sts), slip m, M1L from the bar between sts, work all sts as they appear to the end of this needle, needle change, [p1, k1] 5 times, p1, selv st.

Row 2 (WS): Selv st, [k1, p1] 5 times, k1, needle change, work sts as they appear (knitting the knits and purling the purls) to marker, M1R from the bar between sts, slip m, k1, p1, k1 (Shoulder/raglan sts), slip m, p7 (Sleeve), slip m, k1, p1, k1 (Shoulder/raglan sts), slip m, M1L from the bar between sts, purl to m, M1R from the bar between sts, slip m, k1, p1, k1 (Shoulder/raglan sts), slip m, p7 (Sleeve), slip m, k1, p1, k1 (Shoulder/raglan sts), slip m, M1L from the bar between sts, work all sts as they appear to the end of this needle, needle change, [k1, p1] 5 times, k1, selv st.

Now, it's time for the 1st of the 6 buttonholes.

ARE YOU MAKING THIS SWEATER FOR A MAN OR WOMAN?

For a woman's garment, the Right Front is closed over the Left Front. The Button Band on the Right Front of the garment is on top, and the band on the Left Front underneath. This means that the buttonholes will be worked in the interior facing of the Right Front. When it's time to work a buttonhole, work the 12 DPN sts of the interior facing of the Button Band on the Right Front in a RS row (at the end of the row) as follows: Work 5 sts in 1 × 1 ribbing as the sts appear, BO 3 sts, work 3 sts in 1 × 1 ribbing as the sts appear, selv st. In the following WS row, cast on 3 new stitches above the sts bound off in the previous row for the buttonhole and incorporate them into the 1 × 1 ribbing pattern right from the start.

For a man's garment, the Left Front is closed over the Right Front. The Button Band on the Left Front of the garment is on top, and the band on the Right Front underneath. This means that the buttonholes will be worked in the interior facing of the Left Front. When it's time to work a buttonhole, work the 12 DPN sts of the interior facing of the Button Band on the Left Front in a RS row (at the beginning of the row) as follows: Selv st, 3 sts in 1 × 1 ribbing, BO 3 sts, 5 sts in 1 × 1 ribbing as the sts appear. In the following WS row, cast on 3 new stitches above the sts bound off in the previous row for the buttonhole and incorporate them into the 1 × 1 ribbing pattern right from the start.

From here on, work buttonholes as described above into the interior facing of the Button Band evenly spaced 4 in (10 cm) apart from each other. Work the 1st buttonhole in the next RS row, depending on whether working the woman's or man's version either at the end or the beginning of the stitches on the DPN. You will work a total of 6 buttonholes into the Button Band.

Repeat the following 2 rows another 1/3/4/5 time(s):

Row 1 (RS): Selv st, [p1, k1] 5 times, p1, needle change, work sts as they appear (knitting the knits and purling the purls) to marker, M1R from the bar between sts, slip m, p1, k1, p1 (Shoulder/raglan sts), slip m, k7 (Sleeve), slip m, p1, k1, p1 (Shoulder/raglan sts), slip m, M1L from the bar between sts, knit to m, M1R from the bar between sts, slip m, p1, k1, p1 (Shoulder/raglan sts), slip m, k7 (Sleeve), slip m,

p1, k1, p1 (Shoulder/raglan sts), slip m, M1L from the bar between sts, work all sts as they appear to the end of this needle, needle change, [p1, k1] 5 times, p1, selv st.

Row 2 (WS): Selv st, [k1, p1] 5 times, k1, needle change, work sts as they appear (knitting the knits and purling the purls) to marker, M1R from the bar between sts, slip m, k1, p1, k1 (Shoulder/raglan sts), slip m, p7 (Sleeve), slip m, k1, p1, k1 (Shoulder/raglan sts), slip m, M1L from the bar between sts, purl to m, M1R from the bar between sts, slip m, k1, p1, k1 (Shoulder/raglan sts), slip m, p7 (Sleeve), slip m, k1, p1, k1 (Shoulder/raglan sts), slip m, M1L from the bar between sts, work all sts as they appear to the end of this needle, needle change, [k1, p1] 5 times, k1, selv st.

The Shoulder increases have now been completed. There are 177/199/213/227 sts on the needles: 12 sts each on DPNs, 36/42/46/50 sts for the Front, 5 sts for each Sleeve, 59/69/75/81 sts for the Back, and 3 Shoulder/raglan sts each.

Now it's time for the Sleeve increases. These are worked in every other row, always in a RS row. Repeat the following 2 rows 18/22/22/22 times:

Row 1 (RS): Selv st, [p1, k1] 5 times, p1, needle change, work sts as they appear (knitting the knits and purling the purls) to marker, slip m, p1, k1, p1 (Shoulder/raglan sts), slip m, M1L from the bar between sts, knit to m, M1R from the bar between sts, slip m, p1, k1, p1 (Shoulder/raglan sts), slip m, knit to m, slip m, p1, k1, p1 (Shoulder/raglan sts), slip m, M1L from the bar between sts, knit to m, M1R from the bar between sts, slip m, p1, k1, p1 (Shoulder/raglan sts), slip m, work all sts as they appear to the end of this needle, needle change, [p1, k1] 5 times, p1, selv st.

Row 2 (WS): Work all sts as they appear (knitting the knits and purling the purls), slipping all markers when you encounter them.

Sleeve increases have now been completed. There are 249/287/301/315 sts on the needles: 12 sts on DPNs, 36/42/46/50 sts for the Front, 41/49/49/49 sts for each Sleeve, 59/69/75/81 sts for the Back, and 3 Shoulder/raglan sts each.

Please note: Don't forget to work the buttonholes into the interior facing in evenly spaced intervals.

Now it's time for raglan increases. These are likewise worked in every other row, always in a RS row. Repeat the following 2 rows 6/6/8/12 times:

Row 1 (RS): Selv st, [p1, k1] 5 times, p1, needle change, work sts as they appear (knitting the knits and purling the purls) to marker, M1R from the bar between sts, slip m, p1, k1, p1 (Shoulder/raglan sts), slip m, M1L from the bar between sts, knit to m, M1R from the bar between sts, slip m, p1, k1, p1 (Shoulder/raglan sts), slip m, M1L from the bar between sts, knit to m, M1R from the bar between sts, slip m, p1, k1, p1 (Shoulder/raglan sts), slip m, M1L from the bar between sts, knit to m, M1R from the bar between sts, slip m, p1, k1, p1 (Shoulder/raglan sts), slip m, M1L from the bar between sts, work all sts as they appear to the end of this needle, needle change, [p1, k1] 5 times, p1, selv st.

Row 2 (WS): Work all sts as they appear (knitting the knits and purling the purls), slipping all markers when you encounter them.

All raglan increases have now been completed. There are 297/335/365/411 sts on the needles: 12 sts each on DPNs, 42/48/54/62 sts for the Front, 53/61/65/73 sts for each Sleeve, 71/81/91/105 sts for the Back, and 3 Shoulder/raglan sts each.

Now, the Sleeve stitches will be placed on hold. Shoulder/raglan sts are reallocated to the Body.

RS Row: Work all sts as they appear (knitting the knits and purling the purls) to the 1st marker, slip m, p1, k1, p1, remove m, place 53/61/65/73 sts on holders, CO 5 new underarm sts, remove m, p1, k1, p1, slip m, knit to marker, slip m, p1, k1, p1, remove m, place 53/61/65/73 sts on holders, CO 5 new underarm sts, remove m, p1, k1, p1, slip m, work the remaining sts of this row as they appear.

For the Body, you now have 201/223/245/275 sts on the needles (including the 12 sts each on DPNs).

The newly cast-on sts will be worked in 1 × 1 ribbing, resulting in an 11-sts-wide strip in 1 × 1 ribbing at both imagined side seams. The 4 markers in the knitting set these strips apart; always slip these markers when you encounter them.

Work all sts as they appear in turned rows until work measures 15/15.75/16.5/17.25 in (38/40/42/44 cm) from the transition from the Shoulders to the Collar. Don't forget to work the buttonholes in evenly spaced intervals.

Now, it's time to work the Pocket Slits.

Pocket Slits

For the Pocket Slits, divide the knitted piece into 3 sections and work these separately heightwise: the Left Front, the Right Front, and the combined Sides/Back. Begin at the Left Front edge and first work the 12 DPN sts, then work an additional 20/22/24/26 sts as they appear. Kfb, turn work. Work a WS row using a new, spare needle, over all stitches.

You now have 22/24/26/28 sts on a separate needle plus the established 12 DPN sts. Set the remaining stitches temporarily aside. Over the 22/24/26/28 sts from the separate needle, work 4.25/4.25/4.75/4.75 in (11/11/12/12 cm) in stockinette stitch in turned rows, ending this part with a WS row. Transfer the stitches to a spare needle, extra cord, or piece of waste yarn for holding.

Now, continue the combined Sides/Back as follows: Join new working yarn and begin by working a RS row over the previously held stitches. Kfb in the 1st st, k133/151/169/195, kfb, and turn work. Take up another spare needle and work a WS row over the just-worked stitches. On this new needle, you now have 137/155/173/199 sts. Over these sts, now likewise work 4.25/4.25/4.75/4.75 in (11/11/12/12 cm) in stockinette stitch in turned rows, ending with a WS row. Transfer the stitches to a spare needle, extra cord, or piece of waste yarn for holding.

Now, complete the Right Front as follows: Join new working yarn, and begin by working a RS row over the remaining previously held stitches. Kfb in the 1st st, work 20/22/24/26 sts plus the sts from the DPN as they appear. There are 22/24/26/28 sts on the needles. Over these stitches and the 12 sts from the DPN, now likewise work 4.25/4.25/4.75/4.75 in (11/11/12/12 cm) in stockinette stitch in turned rows, ending with a WS row. Break the working yarn.

Join new working yarn and begin a complete RS row at the Left Front edge. In this RS row, the previously doubled stitches (kfb/pfb) will be knit together again, and work will be joined into the round again.

RS Row: Work 12 DPN sts as they appear, needle change, work 20/22/24/26 sts as they appear (Left Front), ssk, k2tog, work 133/151/169/195 sts as they appear (Sides/Back), ssk, k2tog, work 20/22/24/26 sts as they appear (Right Front), needle change, work 12 DPN sts as they appear. You now have again 177/199/

221/251 sts on the needles plus 12 DPN sts each (= 201/223/245/275 sts).

Then, work 3.25 in (8 cm) in stockinette stitch in turned rows, working all sts as they appear (knitting on the RS and purling on the WS), ending with a WS row.

Now it's time to shape the bottom edge of the Body with wrap and turn short rows (pages 14–15). Work starts on the Left Front:

RS Row: Work all sts as they appear (knitting the knits and purling the purls) to 3 sts before the 1st marker, turn work.

WS Row: Work all sts as they appear to the end of the (short) row.

Work 9/9/11/11 more turns in the established manner, always turning 2 sts before the previous turning point. The 1st part of the short row shaping has been completed.

Now, continue working on the Back:

RS Row: Knit to 1st marker, slip m, work 11 sts in 1 × 1 ribbing, slip m, knit to 3 sts before next m, turn work.

WS Row: Work all sts as they appear to 3 sts before next m, turn work.

Work 9/9/11/11 more turns in the established manner, always turning 2 sts before the previous turning point.

Finally, work the Right Front as follows:

RS Row (this RS row begins on the Back after the last turning point): Knit to next marker, slip m, work 11 sts in 1 × 1 ribbing, slip m, work all sts as they appear (knitting the knits and purling the purls) to end of row.

WS Row: Work all sts as they appear to 3 sts before next m, turn work.

RS Row: Work all sts as they appear to end of row. Repeat the last 2 rows another 9/9/11/11 times, always turning 2 sts before the last turning point.

Please note: On the Right Front, turn after having completed the WS row!

After having completed the last turn, work a WS row, working all sts as they appear. Now, all wraps of the turning stitches have been incorporated.

Begin working the 1 × 1 ribbing pattern: Selv st, [p1, k1] to last 2 sts, p1, selv st. Work an additional 3 rows, working all sts as they appear (knitting the knits and

purling the purls). Bind off all sts using the Italian bind-off method (page 29).

Sleeves

Place the 53/61/65/73 previously held sts of the 1st Sleeve onto a circular needle in size US 8 (5.0 mm), 16 in (40 cm) long, and work 5 sts into the newly cast-on underarm stitches (= 58/66/70/78 sts). Place a marker for the BoR after 2 of the 5 sts.

Now work in stockinette stitch in the round, at the same time working Sleeve tapering decreases at the underside of the Sleeve in every 9th/9th/8th/8th rnd, 8/8/9/9 times in all.

Work **Sleeve tapering decrease round** as follows: K1, ssk, work all sts as they appear to last 3 sts, k2tog, k1.

After having completed 8/8/9/9 decreases, a total of 72/72/72/72 rounds have been worked. The Sleeve has now reached a length of approx. 11 in (28 cm). There are 42/50/52/60 sts on the needles.

Left Sleeve

Now the slit will be worked. Knit to last 25 sts, p1, k1, p1, k2, p1, k1, p1. Knit the remaining sts of the round. Repeat this round an additional 4 times.

From here on, continue in turned rows as follows: Knit to last 25 sts, p1, k1, p1, kfb. Turn work. Work a WS row over all stitches on the needles as they appear, pfb into the last st. Remove the previous marker for the BoR. There are 44/52/54/62 sts on the needles.

Work in stockinette stitch in turned rows with 1 × 1 ribbing at the edges, working all sts as they appear (knitting the knits and purling the purls), until the slit has reached a length of 4 in (10 cm), ending this part with a WS row. At this point, the Sleeve can be lengthened or shortened according to your personal preferences.

Change to size US 6 (4.0 mm) needles and work 0.5 in (1.5 cm) in 1 × 1 ribbing. End this part with a WS row.

Work a buttonhole as follows:

RS Row: Selv st, work all sts as they appear to last 8 sts, BO 3 sts, work 4 sts as they appear, selv st.

In the following WS row, CO 3 new sts over the sts bound off for the buttonhole.

Work an additional 0.75 in (2 cm) in 1 × 1 ribbing, working all sts as they appear. Bind off all sts using the Italian bind-off method (page 29).

Right Sleeve

For the slit, k17, p1, k1, p1, k2, p1, k1, p1. Knit the remaining sts of the round. Repeat this round an additional 4 times, working all sts as they appear (knitting the knits and purling the purls).

From here on, continue in turned rows as follows: K17, p1, k1, p1, kfb. Turn work. Work a WS row over all stitches on the needles as they appear, pfb into the last st. Remove the previous marker for the BoR. There are 44/52/54/62 sts on the needles.

Work in stockinette stitch in turned rows with 1 × 1 ribbing at the edges, working all sts as they appear, until the slit has reached a length of 4 in (10 cm), ending this part with a WS row. At this point, the Sleeve can be lengthened or shortened according to your personal preferences.

Change to US 6 (4.0 mm) needles and work 0.5 in (1.5 cm) in 1 × 1 ribbing.

Work a buttonhole as follows:

RS Row: Selv st, work 4 sts as they appear, BO 3 sts, work the remaining sts as they appear.

In the following WS row, CO 3 new sts over the sts bound off for the buttonhole.

Work an additional 0.75 in (2 cm) in 1 × 1 ribbing, working all sts as they appear. Bind off all sts using the Italian bind-off method (page 29).

Pocket Plackets

The Pocket Plackets in 1 × 1 ribbing will be knitted onto the existing piece. For this, using US 6 (4.0 mm) needles, pick up and work a total of 31/31/33/33 sts from the side of the 1st Pocket Slit facing the front edge as follows:

Row 1 (WS): Selv st, [p1, k1] to last 2 sts, p1, selv st.

Please note: Selv sts located in the Pocket Slits are worked as described on page 68.

Work 1.25 in (3.5 cm) in 1 × 1 ribbing, working all sts as they appear (knitting the knits and purling the purls). Bind off all sts using the Italian bind-off method (page 29).

Work the 2nd Pocket Placket mirror-inverted to the 1st.

Pocket Lining

I recommend working the Pocket Lining using US 6 (4.0 mm) needles and Lamana Como held single, so they turn out thinner and have less bulk. For this, using the US 6 (4.0 mm) DPN set and a single strand of Lamana Como, pick up and knit a total of 62/62/

66/66 sts from the 1st Pocket Slit. Begin at the bottom corner of the slit and work upward along 1 side then back downward along the other side. Join to work in the round and place a marker for the BoR.

Work 4.25 in (11 cm) in stockinette stitch in the round. Then turn the Pocket Lining inside out, so that the WS of the fabric faces you. Place 31/31/33/33 sts each for each side on 2 separate needles held parallel and bind off the Pocket Lining sts from both needles together using the 3-needle-bind-off method (page 30).

Work the 2nd Pocket Lining the same way.

Finishing

Weave in all ends. Sew on the interior facings of the Button Band with small, dot-like, neat stitches and sew on the buttons. Attach the 2 buttons at the Sleeve cuffs, too. After this, attach the Pocket Plackets at the outer corners with 2 small, neat stitches each.

Soak the jacket in lukewarm water with a mild wool detergent. Block it spread out flat on an even, horizontal surface, and let it dry.

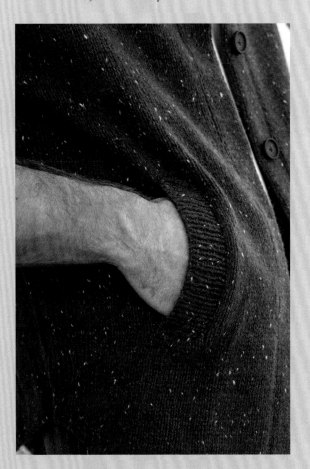

Jesse

Jesse is a simple, everyday sweater that works up quickly. Thanks to its distinctive details and the beautifully shaped collar, this garment is something unique and should not be missing from any closet!

MATERIALS

· Lang Yarns Cashmere Classic; worsted weight; 100% cashmere; 55 yds (50 m) per 0.9 oz (25 g); in 722.0022 Beige Heathered: 17/18/19/20/22/24/27 skeins
Total yardage required: 930/984/1,038/1,094/1,203/1,312/1,476 yds (850/900/950/1,000/1,100/1,200/1,350 m)
· Circular knitting needles in size US 10 (6.0 mm), 24 in (60 cm), 32 in (80 cm), and 40/48 in (100/120 cm) long
· Circular knitting needles in size US 8 (5.0 mm), 16 in (40 cm) and 32/40 in (80/100 cm) long
· DPN sets in size US 8 (5.0 mm) and US 10 (6.0 mm)
· Tapestry needle for weaving in ends
· Stitch markers

SIZES

1/2/3/4/5/6/7
Incorporated positive ease: 4–7 in (10–18 cm)
Chest circumference: 36.5/38.5/41.75/44/47.25/51.25/55.5 in (93/98/106/112/120/130/141 cm)
Upper arm circumference: 13/13.75/14.25/15/16.25/17.25/18 in (33/35/36/38/41/44/46 cm)
Length: 20.5/20.75/21.25/21.75/22/22.5/22.75 in (52/53/54/55/56/57/58 cm)
Our model wears size 3 (Women's M / Men's S)

GAUGE

15 sts and 22 rows = 4 × 4 in (10 × 10 cm) in stockinette stitch on US 10 (6.0 mm) needles (after washing and blocking)

STITCH PATTERNS

Stockinette stitch in turned rows
RS Rows: Knit all stitches.
WS Rows: Purl all sts.

Stockinette stitch in the round
Knit all stitches.

Selvedge stitches
Knit all selvedge stitches in all RS and WS rows.

1 × 1 ribbing for bottom edge and Collar
Alternate knit 1, purl 1.

Shoulder stitches
The 3 Shoulder stitches are set up as "purl 1, knit 1, purl 1" in the beginning, and always worked as the stitches appear. At the beginning of the Sleeve increases, they will be divided, with the knit stitch in the middle being assigned to the Sleeve and the purl stitches at the sides continuing to be worked in purl. During raglan increases, too, and until the Sleeve stitches are placed on hold, these stitches will continue to be purled.

CONSTRUCTION NOTES

The sweater is worked seamlessly from the top down in one piece. Work starts in turned rows, and Shoulder increases are worked to shape Front and Back. At the same time as forming the Sleeves with Sleeve increases, the neckline is shaped before work is joined into the round in the center front. Working in stockinette stitch in the round, Sleeve increases alone are worked first, followed by combined Sleeve and raglan increases. After the Sleeve stitches have been placed on hold, first the Body is completed in the round, then the Sleeves. Both bottom edge and Sleeve cuffs are worked in 1 × 1 ribbing.

Basic Sweater in Stockinette Stitch

REGULAR FIT

LET'S START

Yoke

Using US 10 (6.0 mm) needles, 24 in (60 cm) long, and stretchy cast-on method, cast on 35/35/39/39/39/43/43 sts.

Row 1 is a WS row. Place 4 markers to divide the row into sections as follows: Selv st, p1 (Front), place m, k1, p1, k1 (Shoulder sts), place m, p25/25/29/29/29/33/33 (Back), place m, k1, p1, k1 (Shoulder sts), place m, p1 (Front), selv st.

As described earlier, this has correctly established the Shoulder stitches, which from here on will be worked in every row as they appear (knitting the knits and purling the purls).

Now, in every row (RS and WS rows), increases will be worked before and after the 3 Shoulder stitches, a total of 10/10/10/10/12/12/14 times. Work the following 2 rows 5/5/5/5/6/6/7 times in all:

RS Row: Selv st, knit to m, M1R from the bar between sts, slip m, work the 3 Shoulder stitches as they appear, slip m, M1L from the bar between sts, knit to m, M1R from the bar between sts, slip m, work the 3 Shoulder stitches as they appear, slip m, M1L from the bar between sts, knit to last stitch, selv st.

WS Row: Selv st, purl to m, M1R from the bar between sts, slip m, work the 3 Shoulder stitches as they appear, slip m, M1L from the bar between sts, purl to m, M1R from the bar between sts, slip m, work the 3 Shoulder stitches as they appear, slip m, M1L from the bar between sts, purl to last stitch, selv st.

You have now completed 10/10/10/10/12/12/14 increase rows, during which you have increased a total of 40/40/40/40/48/48/56 sts. There are 75/75/79/79/87/91/99 sts on the needles: 45/45/49/49/53/57/61 sts for the Back, 12/12/12/12/14/14/16 sts each for the 2 Fronts, and 3 Shoulder stitches each for the 2 sides.

Now, in every other row, always in a RS row, Sleeve increases will be worked within the Shoulder stitches a total of 13/12/12/12/13/13/13 times. At the same time, increases to shape the neck opening at the Fronts will be worked.

Row 1 (RS): Selv st, k3, M1L from the bar between sts (neckline increase), knit to m, slip m, p1, M1L from the bar between sts (Sleeve increase), knit to 1 st before the next m, M1R from the bar between sts (Sleeve increase), p1, slip m, knit to next m, slip m, p1, M1L from the bar between sts (Sleeve increase), knit to 1 st before the next m, M1R from the bar between sts (Sleeve increase), p1, slip m, knit to last 4 sts, M1R from the bar between sts (neckline increase), k3, selv st.

Row 2 (WS): Work all sts as they appear (knitting the knits and purling the purls), slipping all markers when you encounter them.

Row 3 (RS): Selv st, knit to m, slip m, p1, M1L from the bar between sts (Sleeve increase), knit to 1 st before the next m, M1R from the bar between sts (Sleeve increase), p1, slip m, knit to next m, slip m, p1, M1L from the bar between sts (Sleeve increase), knit to 1 st before the next m, M1R from the bar between sts (Sleeve increase), p1, slip m, knit to last stitch, selv st.

Row 4 (WS): Work as Row 2.

You have now worked 1 neckline increase for each side. For each half of the Front, there are now 13/13/13/13/15/15/17 sts on the needles. You have also worked 2 Sleeve increases in each increase spot. There are 5 Sleeve stitches for each Sleeve on the needles, including the Shoulder stitch in the middle.

Work Rows 1 and 2 as just described a total of 5/5/6/6/6/7/7 times.

You have now completed a total of 6/6/7/7/7/8/8 neckline increases for each side. For each half of the Front, you now have 18/18/19/19/21/22/24 sts on the needles. You have further worked 7/7/8/8/8/9/9 Sleeve increases in each increase spot. For each Sleeve, you have 15/15/17/17/17/19/19 sts on the needles.

Join to work in the round as follows, connecting the 2 halves of the Front by casting on new sts in the center front using the backwards-loop cast-on method (page 9): Selv st, knit to m, slip m, p1, M1L from the bar between sts (Sleeve increase), knit to 1 st before the next m, M1R from the bar between sts (Sleeve increase), p1, slip m, knit to m, slip m, p1, M1L from the bar between sts (Sleeve increase), knit to 1 st before the next m, M1R from the bar between sts (Sleeve increase), p1, slip m, knit to end of row. Now extend the row by casting on 9/9/11/11/11/13/13 new sts and join into the round. Knit to m—this will be the new BoR. Work 1 round, all sts as they appear (knitting the knits and purling the purls), slipping all markers when you encounter them.

To finish the Sleeve increases on their own, work the following 2 rounds 5/4/3/3/4/3/3 times:

Rnd 1: Slip BoR marker, p1, M1L from the bar between sts, knit to 1 st before the m, M1R from the bar between sts, p1, slip m, knit to next m, slip m, p1, M1L from the bar between sts, knit to 1 st before the m, M1R from the bar between sts, p1, slip m, knit to BoR marker.

Rnd 2: Work all sts as they appear, slipping all markers when you encounter them.

You have now completed a total of 13/12/12/12/13/13/13 Sleeve increases in each increase spot. For the Sleeves, there are now 27/25/25/25/27/27/27 sts on the needles, including the middle Shoulder stitch.

From here on, classic raglan increases will be worked in every other round. Work the following 2 rounds 9/11/12/14/15/17/19 times:

Rnd 1: M1R from the bar between sts, slip BoR marker, p1, M1L from the bar between sts, knit to 1 st before the m, M1R from the bar between sts, p1, slip m, M1L from the bar between sts, knit to next m, M1R from the bar between sts, slip m, p1, M1L from the bar between sts, knit to 1 st before the m, M1R from the bar between sts, p1, slip m, M1L from the bar between sts, knit to BoR marker.

Rnd 2: Work all sts as they appear, slipping all markers when you encounter them.

You have now completed a total of 22/23/24/26/28/30/32 Sleeve increases, 9/11/12/14/15/17/19 as classic raglan increases. There are 220/232/248/264/284/308/332 sts on the needles: 63/67/73/77/83/91/99 sts each for Front and Back, 45/47/49/53/57/61/65 sts for each Sleeve, and 4 purl sts each between Front or Back and Sleeve.

Sleeve stitches are now placed on hold.

Body

Slip BoR marker, p1, transfer the next 45/47/49/53/57/61/65 sts to a spare needle, stitch holder, or piece of waste yarn for holding, CO 5 new underarm sts, p1, remove m, k63/67/73/77/83/91/99, remove m, p1, transfer the next 45/47/49/53/57/61/65 sts to a spare needle, stitch holder, or piece of waste yarn for holding, CO 5 new underarm sts, p1, remove m, k63/67/73/77/83/91/99. For the Body, there are now 140/148/160/168/180/196/212 sts on the needles.

The newly cast-on underarm stitches will be worked in 1 × 1 ribbing as [k1, p1] twice, k1. The previously always purled sts (remainder of the initial Shoulder sts) separating the Front, Back, and Sleeves will continue to be purled. This creates a 7-st-wide strip in 1 × 1 ribbing at the imagined side seam. These sts are worked as they appear (knitting the knits and purling the purls) to the bottom ribbing; the remainder of the Body (Front and Back) is worked in stockinette stitch. Work all sts in the round as they appear, until the Body measures 18/18.5/19/19.25/19.75/20/20.5 in (46/47/48/49/50/51/52 cm) from the transition from the Shoulder to the neck opening. Change to US 8 (5.0 mm) needles and work 2.25 in (6 cm) in 1 × 1 ribbing, beginning with p1. Bind off all sts using the Italian bind-off method (page 29).

Sleeves

Place the 45/47/49/53/57/61/65 previously held sts of the 1st Sleeve onto a circular knitting needle in size US 10 (6.0 mm), 16 in (40 cm) long, and pick up and knit 5 sts from the newly cast-on underarm stitches (= 50/52/54/58/62/66/70 sts). Place a marker for the BoR after 2 of the 5 sts.

Work stockinette stitch in the round, at the same time working Sleeve tapering decreases at the underside of the Sleeve in every 14th/14th/12th/10th/9th/8th/8th rnd a total of 5/5/6/7/8/9/10 times.

Work **Sleeve tapering decrease round** as follows: K1, ssk, work all sts as they appear to last 3 sts, k2tog, k1.

After having completed 5/5/6/7/8/9/10 decreases, a total of 70/70/72/70/72/72/80 rounds have been worked. The Sleeve has now reached a length of 12.5/12.5/13/12.5/13/13/14.25 in (32/32/33/32/33/33/36 cm). You now have a total of 40/42/42/44/46/48/50 sts on the needles.

Continue in stockinette stitch in the round until the Sleeve measures from the armhole 14.25/14.5/15/15.25/15.75/16.25/16.5 in (36/37/38/39/40/41/42 cm). At this point, the Sleeve can be lengthened or shortened according to your personal preferences.

Change to US 8 (5.0 mm) needles and work 2.25 in (6 cm) in 1 × 1 ribbing. Bind off all sts using the Italian bind-off method (page 29).

Work the 2nd Sleeve the same way.

Finishing

Weave in all ends and wash the sweater in lukewarm water with a mild wool detergent. Block it spread out flat on an even, horizontal surface, and let it dry.

Karli

Karli is an absolute must-have garment! This Brioche pattern pullover can be combined elegantly with narrow slacks and a blazer, but it is also the perfect piece to be worn with jeans and sneakers. Worked in the original yarn, the sweater turns out light as a feather and is so soft on the skin!

MATERIALS
· 1 strand Lamana Como; DK weight; 100% extra fine merino wool; 131 yds (120 m) per 0.9 oz (25 g); in 62 Rose Quartz: 12/13/14/15/16/18/19 skeins *held together with*
1 strand Lamana Modena; fingering weight; 70% extra fine merino; 30% cashmere; 366 yds (335 m) per 0.9 oz (25 g) yardage; in 62 Rose Quartz: 5/5/5/6/6/7/7 skeins
Total yardage required: 1,531/1,640/1,750/1,914/2,078/2,242/2,406 yds (1,400/1,500/1,600/1,750/1,900/2,050/2,200 m)
Modifying the length of the garment will change the total yarn requirements accordingly.
· Circular knitting needles in size US 7 (4.5 mm), 16 in (40 cm), 24 in (60 cm), 32 in (80 cm), and 40/48 in (100/120 cm) long
· Circular knitting needles in size US 6 (4.0 mm), 16 in (40 cm) and 32 in (80 cm) long
· DPN sets in sizes US 6 (4.0 mm) and US 7 (4.5 mm)
· Tapestry needle for weaving in ends
· Stitch markers

SIZES
1/2/3/4/5/6/7
Incorporated positive ease: 3.25–4.75 in (8–12 cm)
Chest circumference: 37/38.25/40.5/42.5/45/48.75/52.5 in (94/97/103/108/114/124/133 cm)
Upper arm circumference: 17.25/18/18.5/19.25/19.75/21.25/22 in (44/46/47/49/50/54/56 cm)
Length: 19/19.25/19.75/20/20.5/20.75/21.25 in (48/49/50/51/52/53/54 cm)
Our model wears size 4 (Women's L / Men's M)

GAUGE
17 sts and 36 rows (= 18 Brioche rows) = 4 × 4 in (10 × 10 cm) with 1 of each strand of yarn held together in Brioche pattern on US 7 (4.5 mm) needles (after washing and blocking)

STITCH PATTERNS
Brioche Pattern in turned rows
RS Row: *P1, k1 (working sl1-yo's of previous row together as 1 st as st appears), rep from * to end of row.
WS Row: *K1, sl1-yo (see page 31), rep from * to end of row.

Brioche Pattern in the round
Rnd 1: *K1, p1 (working sl1-yo's of previous row together as 1 stitch as st appears), rep from * around.
Rnd 2: *Sl1-yo (see page 31), p1, rep from * around.

1 × 1 ribbing for Collar and bottom edge
Alternate knit 1, purl 1.

CONSTRUCTION NOTES
Work starts at the top of the Back, with Shoulder increases worked first, followed by armhole increases and placing the Upper Back sts on hold. Stitches for the Left Front are picked up first, then stitches for the Right Front, and both Fronts are shaped with Shoulder decreases and neckline increases. After this, both Fronts are joined, then armhole increases are worked before work is joined into the round and the Body worked in the round in Brioche Pattern. Finally, Sleeve stitches are picked up around the armholes, the Sleeve cap is shaped with short rows, and the Sleeves are completed in Brioche Pattern in the round with Sleeve tapering decreases at the underside of the Sleeve and Sleeve cuffs in a 1 × 1 ribbing pattern.
See tutorials on Brioche Increase and Brioche Decrease on pages 24 and 27.
Work with 1 strand of each yarn held together throughout.

REGULAR FIT

LET'S START

Note: Work with 1 strand of each yarn held together throughout.

Upper Back

Using US 7 (4.5 mm) needles, 24 in (60 cm) long, and stretchy cast-on method, cast on 27/29/31/33/35/39/43 sts.

Setup row is a WS row. Place 2 markers and set up Brioche Pattern as follows: Selv st, [sl1-yo, k1] twice, place m, [sl1-yo, k1] to last 6 sts, sl1-yo, place m, [k1, sl1-yo] twice, selv st.

From here on, increases will be worked immediately adjacent to the markers in every 4th row, always in a RS row. Work the following 4 rows a total of 9/9/10/10/11/11/12 times:

Row 1 (RS): Selv st, work 4 sts in Brioche Pattern as they appear, slip m, Brioche-inc, work Brioche sts as they appear to 1 st before the marker, Brioche-inc, slip m, work 4 sts in Brioche Pattern as they appear, selv st.

Rows 2–4: Work in Brioche Pattern as established.

You have now increased 18/18/20/20/22/22/24 sts on each side. There are 63/65/71/73/79/83/91 sts on the needles in all.

Work 1.25/1.5/1.25/1.5/1.5/1.5/1.5 in (3/4/3/4/4/4/4 cm) in Brioche Pattern, working all sts as they appear. End this part with a WS row.

Now, armhole increases will be worked in every 6th row, always in a RS row. Work the following 6 rows a total of 4/4/4/4/4/5/5 times:

Row 1 (RS): Selv st, work 4 sts in Brioche pattern as they appear, slip m, Brioche-inc, work Brioche sts as they appear to 1 st before the marker, Brioche-inc, slip m, work 4 sts in Brioche pattern as they appear, selv st.

Rows 2–6: Work all Brioche sts as they appear.

You have now increased 8/8/8/8/8/10/10 sts on each side. There are 79/81/87/89/95/103/111 sts on the needles in all.

Break the working yarn and transfer these stitches to a piece of waste yarn, an extra needle, or a spare cord for holding.

Upper Left Front

For this part, pick up and knit 19/19/21/21/23/23/25 sts from the slanted section of the Back Left Shoulder. Begin picking up at the neckline opening and pick up 1 st from every selvedge stitch of the Back. Finish picking up at the Shoulder point of the armhole.

Row 1 is a WS row. Place 2 markers and set up Brioche pattern as follows: Selv st, [sl1-yo, k1] twice, place m, [sl1-yo, k1] to last 6 sts, sl1-yo, place m, [k1, sl1-yo] twice, selv st.

Rows 2–11: Work in Brioche Pattern as sts appear.

On the Front, you will now work decreases on the Shoulder side and neckline increases at the neck side. Please note that only RS rows are written out in the following instructions. In WS rows, all stitches are worked as they appear.

Row 12: Selv st, work in Brioche Pattern to 3 sts before the 2nd m, k3tog, slip m, 4 Brioche sts, selv st.

Row 14: Work all Brioche sts as they appear.

Row 16: Selv st, 4 Brioche sts, slip m, Brioche-inc, work all remaining sts in Brioche pattern.

Rows 18, 20, 26, 30: Work as Row 14.

Row 22, 28, 32: Work as Row 16.

Row 24: Work as Row 12.

Rows 34: Work as Row 14.

You have now worked 2 decreases on the Shoulder side and have already completed 4 increases at the neckline side.

Work the following 4 rows a total of 0/0/1/1/2/2/2 time(s):

Row 1 (RS): Selv st, 4 Brioche sts, slip m, Brioche-inc, work all remaining sts in Brioche pattern.

Rows 2–4: Work all Brioche sts as they appear. Neckline increases for all sizes have now been completed. There are 23/23/27/27/31/31/33 sts on the needles. Break the working yarn and set these stitches temporarily aside on a spare needle or cord.

Upper Right Front

For this part, pick up and knit 19/19/21/21/23/23/25 sts from the slanted section of the Back Right Shoulder. Begin picking up at the Shoulder point of the armhole and pick up 1 st from every selvedge stitch of the Back. Finish picking up at the neckline opening.

Row 1 is a WS row. Place 2 markers and set up Brioche Pattern as follows: Selv st, [sl1-yo, k1] twice, place m, [sl1-yo, k1] to last 6 sts, sl1-yo, place m, [k1, sl1-yo] twice, selv st.

Rows 2–11: Work all Brioche sts as they appear.

On the Front, you will now work decreases on the Shoulder side and neckline increases at the neck side. Please note that only RS rows are written out in the following instructions. In WS rows, all stitches are worked as they appear.

Row 12: Selv st, 4 Brioche sts, slip m, sssk, work remaining sts in Brioche Pattern, selv st.

Row 14: Work all Brioche sts as they appear.

Row 16: Selv st, all sts in Brioche Pattern to 1 st before the 2nd m, Brioche-inc, slip m, 4 Brioche sts, selv st.

Rows 18, 20, 26, 30: Work as Row 14.

Row 22, 28, 32: Work as Row 16.

Row 24: Work as Row 12.

Rows 34: Work as Row 14.

You have now worked 2 decreases on the Shoulder side and have already completed 4 increases at the neckline side.

Work the following 4 rows a total of 0/0/1/1/2/2/2 time(s):

Row 1 (RS): Selv st, work all sts in Brioche Pattern to 1 st before the 2nd m, Brioche-inc, slip m, 4 Brioche sts, selv st.

Rows 2–4: Work all sts in Brioche Pattern as they appear.

Neckline increases for all sizes have now been completed. There are 23/23/27/27/31/31/33 sts on the needles now.

The Upper Right Front and the Upper Left Front will be joined as follows:

Work all sts of the Upper Right Front in Brioche Pattern as they appear, extend the row by casting on 9/9/9/11/11/13/15 new sts, then work all sts of the Upper Left Front in Brioche Pattern as they appear. There are 55/55/63/65/73/75/81 sts on the needles in all. Work 1.25/1.5/1.25/1.5/1.5/1.5/1.5 in (3/4/3/4/4/4/4 cm) in Brioche pattern in turned rows, working all sts as they appear (Brioche-knitting the knits and Brioche-purling the purls). Incorporate the newly cast-on sts in the center front into the stitch pattern from the 1st WS row on, ending this part with a WS row.

Now, armhole increases will be worked in every 6th row, always in a RS row. Work the following 6 rows a total of 4/4/4/4/4/5/5 times:

Row 1 (RS): Selv st, work 4 sts in Brioche Pattern as they appear, slip m, Brioche-inc, work all sts in Brioche Pattern as they appear to 1 st before the marker, Brioche-inc, slip m, work 4 sts in Brioche Pattern as they appear, selv st.

Rows 2–6: Work all sts in Brioche Pattern as they appear.

You have now increased 8/8/8/8/8/10/10 sts on each side. There are 71/71/79/81/89/95/101 sts on the needles in all.

Body

Now, join to work in the round. Work all 71/71/79/81/89/95/101 sts of the Front in Brioche Pattern as they appear, cast on 5/7/5/7/5/7/7 new sts, work all 79/81/87/89/95/103/111 sts of the Back in Brioche Pattern as they appear, cast on 5/7/5/7/5/7/7 new sts. After having worked 4 of the newly cast-on sts, place a marker for the BoR. The new BoR will from here on be located at the right underarm, the 1st st of the round will be a Brioche knit stitch. Incorporate the newly cast-on underarm sts into the stitch pattern right from the beginning.

Work in Brioche Pattern in the round until the sweater measures 16.5/17/17.25/17.75/18/18.5/19 in (42/43/44/45/46/47/48 cm) from the highest point at the Shoulder. End this part with a Rnd 1 of the stitch pattern. Change to US 6 (4.0 mm) needles and work 2.25 in (6 cm) in 1 × 1 ribbing. Bind off all sts using the Italian bind-off method (page 29).

Sleeves

Pick up and knit a total of 74/76/78/82/86/92/96 sts around the 1st armhole at a rate of 1 st picked up from every 2. In Brioche Pattern, "picking up 1 from every 2" means that you will pick up 1 st from every visible

Brioche stitch around the armhole (1 Brioche stitch is always composed of 2 rows of Brioche Pattern). Begin picking up in the center of the underarm sts and work upward over the Shoulder and back down again to the underarm. Join to work in the round and place a marker for the BoR. After the 1st 37/38/39/41/43/46/48 sts, place a marker to denote the Shoulder point.

First, work wrap and turn short rows (pages 14–15) to shape the Sleeve cap as follows:

[Sl1-yo, p1] to 1 st before the Shoulder point marker, sl1-yo, slip m, [p1, sl1-yo] 3 times, p1, turn work.

Work all sts to the Shoulder point marker in the now established Brioche Pattern, slip m, 7 Brioche sts, turn work.

Work 6 more turns for each side, each time working 4 sts past the previous turn; the turning stitch of the previous row will always be the 1st of the 4 sts. Short rows for Sleeve cap shaping have now been completed.

Work in Brioche Pattern in the round with Sleeve tapering decreases at the underside of the Sleeve in every 18th/24th/24th/18th/18th/16th/14th rnd a total of 6/5/5/6/6/7/8 times. Work the **decrease round**, always in a Rnd 1 of the pattern repeat, as follows:
K1, p1, k3tog, work in Brioche Pattern to last 5 sts, sssk, p1, k1.

After having completed 6/5/5/6/6/7/8 decreases, a total of 108/120/120/108/108/112/112 rounds have been worked. The Sleeve has now reached a length of 11.75/13/13/11.75/11.75/12.25/12.25 in (30/33/33/30/30/31/31 cm). There are 50/56/58/58/62/64/64 sts on the needles.

Continue to work in Brioche Pattern in the round until the Sleeve measures 15/15.25/15.75/16.25/16.5/17/17.25 in (38/39/40/41/42/43/44 cm) from the underarm. At this point, the Sleeve can be lengthened or shortened according to your personal preferences. Change to US 6 (4.0 mm) needles and work 2.25 in (6 cm) in 1 × 1 ribbing. Bind off all sts using the Italian bind-off method (page 29).

Work the 2nd Sleeve the same way.

Neckband

Pick up and knit a total of 88/90/98/104/112/118/122 sts around the neckline edge at a ratio of 8 sts picked up from every 9 sts. Beginning in the center Back, pick up 1 st each from every 8 sts, skipping the 9th st. Join to work in the round and place a marker for the BoR. Work 1 rnd in 1 × 1 ribbing.

Begin working wrap and turn short rows (pages 14–15) at the neckband:

Work 36 sts in 1 × 1 ribbing as sts appear; turn work.
Work 72 sts in 1 × 1 ribbing as sts appear; turn work.
Work 64 sts in 1 × 1 ribbing as sts appear; turn work.
Work 56 sts in 1 × 1 ribbing as sts appear; turn work.
Work 48 sts in 1 × 1 ribbing as sts appear; turn work.
Work 40 sts in 1 × 1 ribbing as sts appear; turn work.
Work in 1 × 1 ribbing as sts appear to BoR marker.
Work an additional 12 rnds in 1 × 1 ribbing.
Purl 1 rnd to create a fold line, then work 12 more rnds in 1 × 1 ribbing.
Then, mirror-inverted to the outside of the neckband, work wrap and turn short rows (pages 14–15) as follows:

Work 20 sts in 1 × 1 ribbing as sts appear, turn work.
Work 40 sts in 1 × 1 ribbing as sts appear, turn work.
Work 48 sts in 1 × 1 ribbing as sts appear, turn work.
Work 56 sts in 1 × 1 ribbing as sts appear, turn work.
Work 64 sts in 1 × 1 ribbing as sts appear, turn work.
Work 72 sts in 1 × 1 ribbing as sts appear, turn work.
Work in 1 × 1 ribbing as sts appear to BoR marker, then work an additional full round in 1 × 1 ribbing. Bind off all sts using the Italian bind-off method (page 29).

Finishing

Weave in all ends, fold the neckband to the inside, and sew it on around the pick-up edge with small, neat stitches. Wash the sweater in lukewarm water with a mild wool detergent. Block it spread out flat on an even, horizontal surface, and let it dry.

Quinn

This sweater, with a deep neckline framed by a ribbed neckband, could be a sturdy outdoor garment for your significant other, or turn it into your own favorite piece! Worked in alpaca yarn, it is the perfect companion for the colder season; try it in cotton or bamboo for a summer layer.

MATERIAL
· 1 strand Pascuali Alpaca Fino; DK/light worsted weight; 100% baby alpaca; 109 yd (100 m) per 1.75 oz (50 g); in 04 Medium Taupe: 9/10/11/13/14/16/18 skeins
held together with
1 strand Pascuali Alpaca Lace; lace weight; 100% baby alpaca; 437 yds (400 m) per 1.75 oz (50 g); in 05 Medium Taupe: 3/3/3/4/4/4/5 skeins
Total yardage required: 930/1,038/1,148/1,367/1,531/1,750/1,968.5 yds (850/950/1,050/1,250/1,400/1,600/1,800 m)
· Circular knitting needles in size US 7 (4.5 mm), 16 in (40 cm), 24 in (60 cm), 32 in (80 cm), and 40/48 in (100/120 cm) long
· Circular knitting needles in size US 6 (4.0 mm), 32 in (80 cm) and 40 in (100 cm) long
· DPN sets in size US 6 (4.0 mm) and US 7 (4.5 mm)
· Tapestry needle for weaving in ends
· Stitch markers

SIZES
1/2/3/4/5/6/7
Incorporated positive ease: 4–7 in (10–18 cm)
Chest circumference: 37.75/40.25/43/45.75/48/52/56 in (96/102/109/116/122/132/142 cm)
Upper arm circumference: 12.5/13.5/13.75/15/16.25/17.25/19 in (32/34/35/38/41/44/48 cm)
Length: 20.5/20.75/21.25/21.75/22/22.5/22.75 in (52/53/54/55/56/57/58 cm)
Our model wears size 4 (Women's L / Men's M)

GAUGE
17 sts and 26 rows = 4 × 4 in (10 × 10 cm) in stockinette stitch with 1 strand of each yarn held together on US 7 (4.5 mm) needles (after washing and blocking)

STITCH PATTERNS
Stockinette stitch in turned rows
RS Rows: Knit all stitches.
WS Rows: Purl all sts.

2 × 2 ribbing for Neckband and bottom edge
Alternate knit 2, purl 2.

CONSTRUCTION NOTES
Work starts at the top of the Back, first working Shoulder increases, followed by armhole increases and placing the stitches of the Upper Back on hold. After this, stitches for the Left Front, then stitches for the Right Front are picked up, then both Fronts are worked with Shoulder decreases and shaping increases for the V-neck/ribbed Neckband and the armholes.
After this, both halves of the Front and the Back are joined and worked in stockinette stitch in turned rows with V-neck shaping increases. Then all stitches are placed on hold.
After having worked Ribbed Neckband with short-row shaping, the stitches are bound off and the bottom edges placed atop each other. Work is joined into the round, and the Body is finished in stockinette stitch in the round. The bottom edge, worked in 2 × 2 ribbing, is knitted onto the existing piece. Finally, Sleeve stitches are picked up around the armholes, the Sleeve cap is shaped with short rows, and the Sleeves are worked in stockinette stitch in the round with Sleeve tapering decreases at the underside of the Sleeve and finished with Sleeve cuffs in 2 × 2 ribbing.
Work with 1 strand of each yarn held together throughout.

Pullover with Overlapping V-neckband

RELAXED FIT

LET'S START

Note: Work with 1 strand of each yarn held together throughout.

Upper Back

Using US 7 (4.5 mm) needles, 24 in (60 cm) long, and stretchy cast-on method, cast on 27/29/31/33/35/37/39 sts.

Row 1 is a WS row. Place 2 markers as follows: Selv st, p5, place m, purl to last 6 sts, place m, p5, selv st. From here on, increases will be worked in every row (RS and WS rows) immediately adjacent to the markers. Work the following 2 rows a total of 8/8/9/10/10/11/11 times:

RS Row: Selv st, k5, slip m, M1L from the bar between sts, knit to m, M1R from the bar between sts, slip m, k5, selv st.

WS Row: Selv st, p5, slip m, M1L from the bar between sts, purl to m, M1R from the bar between sts, slip m, p5, selv st.

You have now increased 16/16/18/20/20/22/22 sts on each side. There are 59/61/67/73/75/81/83 sts on the needles in all.

Work 3.5/4/4/4/4/4/4 in (9/10/10/10/10/10/10 cm) in stockinette stitch in turned rows, ending with a WS row. Now armhole increases will be worked in every other row, always in a RS row. Work the following 2 rows a total of 6/7/7/7/8/9/11 times:

RS Row: Selv st, k5, slip m, M1L from the bar between sts, knit to m, M1R from the bar between sts, slip m, k5, selv st.

WS Row: Work all sts as they appear (knitting the knits and purling the purls), slipping all markers when you encounter them.

There are 71/75/81/87/91/99/105 sts on the needles. Break the working yarn and transfer these stitches to a piece of waste yarn, an extra needle, or a spare cord for holding.

Upper Right Front

For this part, pick up 17/17/19/21/21/23/23 sts from the slanted part of the Back Right Shoulder. Begin picking up at the Shoulder point of the armhole and pick up 1 st from every selv st of the Back. Finish picking up at the neckline opening.

Row 1 is a WS row. Place 2 markers as follows: Selv st, p5, place m, purl to last 5 sts, place m, p4, selv st. From here on, V-neck shaping increases will be worked at the left edge of the Right Front in every 4th row (always in a RS row), 14/15/15/15/17/18/19 times in all. At the same time, decreases will be worked at the right edge of the Right Front in every 6th row (always in a RS row), 6 times in all. Please note that only RS rows are written out in the following instructions. In all WS rows, work all sts as they appear (knitting the knits and purling the purls).

Row 2: Work all sts as they appear (knitting the knits and purling the purls).

Row 4: Selv st, knit to 2nd marker, M1R from the bar between sts, slip m, k5, selv st.

Row 6: Selv st, k4, slip m, ssk, knit to end of row.

Row 8: Work as Row 4.

Row 10: Work as Row 2.

Row 12: Selv st, k4, slip m, ssk, knit to next m, M1R from the bar between sts, slip m, k5, selv st.

Rows 14, 22, 26, 34: Work as Row 2.

Rows 16, 20, 28, 32: Work as Row 4.

Rows 18, 30: Work as Row 6.

Rows 24, 36: Work as Row 12.

Row 38: Work as Row 2.

All decreases on the Shoulder side have now been completed. The marker for the Shoulder increases may be removed now.

Up to here, you have worked 9 increases at the V-neck. There are 20/20/22/24/24/26/26 sts on the needles.

Rows 40, 44: Work as Row 4.

Rows 41–43, 45–47: Work as Row 2.

Now, begin working armhole increases at the same time.

Size 1:
Increases will be worked in every other row (always in a RS row) a total of 6 times. Neckline increases will continue to be worked in every 4th row.

Row 48: Selv st, k5, M1L from the bar between sts, knit to m, M1R from the bar between sts, slip m, k5, selv st.

Row 50: Selv st, k5, M1L from the bar between sts, knit to end of row.

Rows 52, 56: Work as Row 48.

Rows 54, 58: Work as Row 50.

Both armhole increases and neckline increases have been completed now. There are 25 sts on the needles. Break the working yarn and transfer these stitches to a piece of waste yarn, an extra needle, or a spare cord for holding.

Sizes 2/3/4:
Increases will be worked in every other row (always in a RS row) a total of 7 times. Neckline increases will continue to be worked in every 4th row.

Row 48: Selv st, k5, M1L from the bar between sts, knit to m, M1R from the bar between sts, slip m, k5, selv st.

Row 50: Selv st, k5, M1L from the bar between sts, knit to end of row.

Rows 52, 56, 60: Work as Row 48.

Rows 54, 58: Work as Row 50.

Both armhole increases and neckline increases have been completed now. There are 26/28/30 sts on the needles.

Break the working yarn and transfer these stitches to a piece of waste yarn, an extra needle, or a spare cord for holding.

Size 5:
Increases will be worked in every other row (always in a RS row) a total of 8 times. Neckline increases will continue to be worked in every 4th row.

Row 48: Selv st, k5, M1L from the bar between sts, knit to m, M1R from the bar between sts, slip m, k5, selv st.

Row 50: Selv st, k5, M1L from the bar between sts, knit to end of row.

Rows 52, 56, 60: Work as Row 48.

Rows 54, 58, 62: Work as Row 50.

Armhole increases have now been completed. So far, you have worked 15 increases at the neck side, 2 more increases still have to be worked. There are 30 sts on the needles. Break the working yarn and transfer these stitches to a piece of waste yarn, an extra needle, or a spare cord for holding.

Size 6:
Increases will be worked in every other row (always in a RS row) a total of 9 times. Neckline increases will continue to be worked in every 4th row.

Row 48: Selv st, k5, M1L from the bar between sts, knit to m, M1R from the bar between sts, slip m, k5, selv st.

Row 50: Selv st, k5, M1L from the bar between sts, knit to end of row.

Rows 52, 56, 60, 64: Work as Row 48.

Rows 54, 58, 62: Work as Row 50.

Armhole increases have now been completed. So far, you have worked 16 increases at the neck side, 2 more increases still have to be worked. There are 33 sts on the needles. Break the working yarn and transfer these stitches to a piece of waste yarn, an extra needle, or a spare cord for holding.

Size 7:
Increases will be worked in every other row (always in a RS row) a total of 11 times. Neckline increases will continue to be worked in every 4th row.

Row 48: Selv st, k5, M1L from the bar between sts, knit to m, M1R from the bar between sts, slip m, k5, selv st.

Row 50: Selv st, k5, M1L from the bar between sts, knit to end of row.

Rows 52, 56, 60, 64, 68: Work as Row 48.

Rows 54, 58, 62. 66: Work as Row 50.

Armhole increases have now been completed. So far, you have worked 17 increases at the neck side, 2 more increases still have to be worked. There are 34 sts on the needles. Break the working yarn and transfer these stitches to a piece of waste yarn, an extra needle, or a spare cord for holding.

Upper Left Front
For this part, pick up and knit 17/17/19/21/21/23/23 sts from the slanted part of the Back Left Shoulder. Begin picking up at the neckline opening and pick up 1 st from every selvedge stitch of the Back. Finish picking up at the Shoulder point of the armhole.

Row 1 is a WS row. Place 2 markers as follows: Selv st, p4, place m, purl to last 6 sts, place m, p5, selv st. From here on, V-neck shaping increases will be worked at the right edge of the Left Front in every 4th row (always in a RS row) a total of 14/15/15/15/17/18/19 times. At the same time, decreases will be worked at the left edge of the Left Front in every 6th row (always in a RS row), 6 times in all. Please note that only RS rows are written out in the following instructions. In all WS rows, work all sts as they appear (knitting the knits and purling the purls).

Row 2: Work all sts as they appear (knitting the knits and purling the purls).

Row 4: Selv st, k5, slip m, M1L from the bar between sts, knit to end of row.

Row 6: Selv st, knit to 2 sts before the 2nd marker, k2tog, slip m, k4, selv st.

Rows 8, 16, 20, 28, 32: Work as Row 4.

Rows 10, 14, 22, 26, 34: Work as Row 2.

Row 12: Selv st, k5, slip m, M1L from the bar between sts, knit to 2 sts before the 2nd marker, k2tog, slip m, k4, selv st.

Row 18, 30: Work as Row 6.

Row 24, 36: Work as Row 12.

Row 38: Work as Row 2.

All decreases on the Shoulder side have now been completed. The marker for the Shoulder increases may be removed.

Up to here, you have worked 9 increases at the V-neck. There are 20/20/22/24/24/26/26 sts on the needles.

Rows 40, 44: Work as Row 4.

Rows 41–43, 45–47: Work as Row 2.

Now, begin working armhole increases at the same time.

Size 1:

Increases will be worked in every other row (always in a RS row) a total of 6 times. Neckline increases will continue to be worked in every 4th row.

Row 48: Selv st, k5, slip m, M1L from the bar between sts, knit to last 6 sts, M1R from the bar between sts, k5, selv st.

Row 50: Selv st, knit to last 6 sts, M1R from the bar between sts, k5, selv st.

Rows 52, 56: Work as Row 48.

Rows 54, 58: Work as Row 50.

Both armhole increases and neckline increases have been completed now. There are 25 sts on the needles.

Sizes 2/3/4:

Increases will be worked in every other row (always in a RS row) a total of 7 times. Neckline increases will continue to be worked in every 4th row.

Row 48: Selv st, k5, slip m, M1L from the bar between sts, knit to last 6 sts, M1R from the bar between sts, k5, selv st.

Row 50: Selv st, knit to last 6 sts, M1R from the bar between sts, k5, selv st.

Rows 52, 56, 60: Work as Row 48.

Rows 54, 58: Work as Row 50.

Both armhole increases and neckline increases have been completed now. There are 26/28/30 sts on the needles.

Size 5:

Increases will be worked in every other row (always in a RS row) a total of 8 times. Neckline increases will continue to be worked in every 4th row.

Row 48: Selv st, k5, slip m, M1L from the bar between sts, knit to last 6 sts, M1R from the bar between sts, k5, selv st.

Row 50: Selv st, knit to last 6 sts, M1R from the bar between sts, k5, selv st.

Rows 52, 56, 60: Work as Row 48.

Rows 54, 58, 62: Work as Row 50.

Armhole increases have now been completed. So far, you have worked 15 increases at the neck side, 2 more increases still have to be worked. There are 30 sts on the needles.

Size 6:

Increases will be worked in every other row (always in a RS row) a total of 9 times. Neckline increases will continue to be worked in every 4th row.

Row 48: Selv st, k5, slip m, M1L from the bar between sts, knit to last 6 sts, M1R from the bar between sts, k5, selv st.

Row 50: Selv st, knit to last 6 sts, M1R from the bar between sts, k5, selv st.

Rows 52, 56, 60, 64: Work as Row 48.

Rows 54, 58, 62: Work as Row 50.

Armhole increases have now been completed. So far, you have worked 16 increases at the neck side, 2 more increases still have to be worked. There are 33 sts on the needles.

Size 7:

Increases will be worked in every other row (always in a RS row) a total of 11 times. Neckline increases will continue to be worked in every 4th row.

Row 48: Selv st, k5, slip m, M1L from the bar between sts, knit to last 6 sts, M1R from the bar between sts, k5, selv st.

Row 50: Selv st, knit to last 6 sts, M1R from the bar between sts, k5, selv st.

Rows 52, 56, 60, 64, 68: Work as Row 48.

Rows 54, 58, 62. 66: Work as Row 50.

Armhole increases have now been completed. So far, you have worked 17 increases at the neck side, 2 more increases still have to be worked. There are 34 sts on the needles.

Continue for Sizes 1/2/3/4:

The Fronts and the Back will be joined as follows:
Knit all 25/26/28/30 sts of the Left Front, CO 5 new underarm sts, knit all 71/75/81/87 sts of the Back, CO 5 new underarm sts, knit all 25/26/28/30 sts of the Right Front.

There are 155/165/175/185 sts on the needles. Work 1.5/2/2.25/2.75 in (4/5/6/7 cm) even in stockinette stitch in turned rows without further increases, ending this part with a WS row.

Continue for Size 5:

The Fronts and the Back will be joined. Additionally, 2 more V-neck increases will be worked.

Row 64: Selv st, k5, slip m, M1L from the bar between sts, knit the remaining sts of the Left Front, CO 5 new underarm sts, knit all 75 sts of the Back, CO 5 new underarm sts, knit the sts of the Right Front to marker, M1R from the bar between sts, slip m, k5, selv st.

Row 66: Work all sts as they appear (knitting the knits and purling the purls).

Row 68: Selv st, k5, slip m, M1L from the bar between sts, knit to next m, M1R from the bar between sts, slip m, k5, selv st.

The increases at the neck side have now been completed. There are 197 sts on the needles. Work 2 in (5 cm) even in stockinette stitch in turned rows without further increases, ending this part with a WS row.

Continue for Size 6:

The Fronts and the Back will be joined. Additionally, 2 more V-neck increases will be worked.

Row 66: Selv st, knit all sts of the Left Front, CO 5 new underarm sts, knit all 81 sts of the Back, CO 5 new underarm sts, knit all sts of the Right Front.

Rows 68, 72: Selv st, k5, slip m, M1L from the bar

between sts, knit to next m, M1R from the bar between sts, slip m, k5, selv st.

Row 70: Work all sts as they appear (knitting the knits and purling the purls).

The increases at the neck side have now been completed. There are 221 sts on the needles. Work 2.25 in (5.5 cm) even in stockinette stitch in turned rows without further increases, ending this part with a WS row.

Continue for Size 7:

The Fronts and the Back will be joined. Additionally, 2 more V-neck increases will be worked.

Row 70: Selv st, knit all sts of the Left Front, CO 5 new underarm sts, knit all 81 sts of the Back, CO 5 new underarm sts, knit all sts of the Right Front.

Rows 72, 76: Selv st, k5, slip m, M1L from the bar between sts, knit to next m, M1R from the bar between sts, slip m, k5, selv st.

Row 74: Work all sts as they appear (knitting the knits and purling the purls).

The increases at the neck side have now been completed. There are 231 sts on the needles. Work 2.25 in (5.5 cm) even in stockinette stitch in turned rows without further increases, ending this part with a WS row.

Ribbed Neckband

Neckline shaping has now been completed. Break the working yarn and place all stitches on hold. The ribbed Neckband will be worked next.

Using a circular needle in size US 6 (4.0 mm), 40 in (100 cm) long, pick up and knit stitches for the Collar along the front edge at a rate of 8 sts picked up from every 9 sts. Start at the bottom edge of the Right Front, work toward the top and across the Back to the bottom edge of the Left Front. Pick up a total of 132/144/148/152/168/180/188 sts this way. If your stitch count is different, make sure it is a multiple of 4.

Row 1 (WS): Selv st, [p2, k2]to last 3 sts, p2, selv st. Work 1.25 in (3.5 cm) in turned rows in 2 × 2 ribbing, working all sts as they appear (knitting the knits and purling the purls). Now, work wrap and turn short rows (pages 14–15) to raise the height of the ribbed neckband in the center Back:

RS Row: Work all sts as they appear (knitting the knits and purling the purls) to last 16 sts; turn work.

WS Row: Work all sts as they appear to last 16 sts; turn work.

RS Row: Work all sts as they appear to last 24 sts; turn work.

WS Row: Work all sts as they appear to last 24 sts; turn work.

RS Row: Work all sts as they appear to last 32 sts; turn work.

WS Row: Work all sts as they appear to last 32 sts; turn work.

RS Row: Work all sts as they appear to last 40 sts; turn work.

WS Row: Work all sts as they appear to last 40 sts; turn work.

RS Row: Work all sts as they appear to last 48 sts; turn work.

WS Row: Work all sts as they appear to last 48 sts; turn work.

RS Row: Work all sts as they appear to last 56 sts; turn work.

WS Row: Work all sts as they appear to last 56 sts; turn work.

RS Row: Work all sts as they appear to last 64 sts; turn work.

WS Row: Work all sts as they appear to last 64 sts; turn work.

RS Row: Work all sts as they appear to last 72 sts; turn work.

WS Row: Work all sts as they appear to last 72 sts; turn work.

Work a RS row over all remaining stitches.

Continue to work in 2 × 2 ribbing, working all sts as they appear, until the Collar measures 3 in (7.5 cm) along the bottom edge. Bind off all stitches.

ARE YOU MAKING THIS SWEATER FOR A MAN OR WOMAN?

For a woman's garment, the Right Front is closed over the Left Front. The part of the Neckband on the Right Front of the garment is on top, and the one on the Left Front is underneath.

For a man's garment, the Left Front is closed over the Right Front. The part of the Neckband on the Left Front of the garment is on top, and the one on the Right Front is underneath.

Therefore, depending on whether you are making this sweater for a man or woman, place the respective top placket on top of the under placket and pin the neckband using tailor pins. Join new working yarn and, using size US 7 (4.5 mm) needles, beginning at the

right edge of the bottom edges, pick up and knit 11 sts from the neckband. Knit 25/26/28/30/32/35/36 sts (the previously held stitches of the Left Front), then place a marker to indicate the BoR. There are 166/176/186/196/208/232/242 sts on the needles. Work in stockinette stitch in the round until the sweater measures 18/18.5/19/19.25/19.75/20/20.5 in (46/47/48/49/50/51/52 cm) from the highest point at the Shoulder (transition between Shoulder and Neckband). Change to US 6 (4.0 mm) needles and work 2.25 in (6 cm) in 2 × 2 ribbing pattern.

For sizes 1, 3, and 7 only: During the 1st round of the neckline ribbing, in 2 spots of your choice, work either k2tog or p2tog (depending on the place in the pattern) for a total of 2 sts decreased.

Sleeves

Pick up and knit a total of 58/60/62/64/66/70/74 sts around the 1st armhole at a rate of 1 st picked up from every 2. Begin picking up in the center of the underarm sts and work upward over the Shoulder and back down again to the underarm. Join to work in the round and place a marker for the BoR. After the 1st 29/30/31/32/33/35/37 sts, place a marker for the Shoulder point.

First, work wrap and turn short rows (pages 14–15) to shape the Sleeve cap as follows:

Knit to Shoulder point marker, slip m, k7, turn work. P7, slip m, p7, turn work.

Following the established sequence, work 8 more turns on each side, always working to 3 sts after the previous turn; the turning stitch of the previous row is always the 1st stitch of the 3 sts. All short rows have been completed now.

Work in stockinette stitch in the round with Sleeve tapering decreases at the underside of the Sleeve in every 16th/18th/16th/18th/16th/16th/12th rnd a total of 5/4/5/4/5/5/7 times.

Work a **decrease round** as follows: K1, k2tog, k to last 3 sts, ssk, k1.

After having completed 5/4/5/4/5/5/7 decreases, a total of 80/72/80/72/80/80/84 rounds have been worked.

The Sleeve has reached a length of 12.25/15/12.25/15/12.25/12.25/12.5 in (31/38/31/38/31/31/32 cm). There are 48/52/52/56/56/60/60 sts on the needles. Continue to work in stockinette stitch in the round until the Sleeve measures 15/15.25/15.75/16.25/16.5/17/17.25 in (38/39/40/41/42/43/44 cm) from the underarm. At this point, the Sleeve can be lengthened or shortened according to your personal preferences. Change to US 6 (4.0 mm) needles and work 2.25 in (6 cm) in 2 × 2 ribbing.

Bind off all stitches. Work the 2nd Sleeve the same way.

Finishing

Weave in all ends and wash the sweater in lukewarm water with a mild wool detergent. Block it spread out flat on an even, horizontal surface, and let it dry.

Lenny

This classy, ribbed sweater with vertical stripes impresses with its partial button band transitioning into a mock turtleneck collar. Combined with jeans, boots, and parka, it will become your perfect companion for the fall!

MATERIALS

· Lang Yarns Merino +; worsted weight; 100% extra fine merino wool; 98.5 yds (90 m) per 1.75 oz (50 g); in 152.0035 Marine: 12/13/14/15/16/18/20 skeins
  Total yardage required: 1,094/1,203/1,312/1,422/
  1,531/1,750/1,968.5 yds (1,000/1,100/1,200/
  1,300/1,400/1,600/1,800 m)
· Circular knitting needles in size US 7 (4.5 mm), 16 in (40 cm), 24 in (60 cm), 32 in (80 cm), and 40/ 48 in (100/120 cm) long
· Circular knitting needles in size US 6 (4.0 mm), 2 each in 24 in (60 cm) and 32/40 in (80/100 cm) long
· DPN sets in size US 6 (4.0 mm) and US 7 (4.5 mm)
· Tapestry needle for weaving in ends
· Stitch markers
· 2 safety pins
· Sewing thread in matching color and sewing needle

SIZES

1/2/3/4/5/6/7
Incorporated positive ease: 4–7 in (10–18 cm)
Chest circumference: 37.75/40.5/43.25/45/47.25/
51.25/56.25 in (96/103/110/114/120/130/143 cm)
Upper arm circumference: 13/14.25/14.25/15.75/17/
17/18 in (33/36/36/40/43/43/46 cm)
Length: 19.75/20/20.5/21/21.25/21.75/22 in (50/51/
52/53/54/55/56 cm)
Our model wears size 4 (Women's L / Men's M)

GAUGE

18 sts and 26 rows = 4 × 4 in (10 × 10 cm) in stockinette stitch on US 7 (4.5 mm) needles (after washing and blocking)

STITCH PATTERNS

2 × 2 ribbing for Mock Turtleneck Collar
Alternate knit 2, purl 2.

1 × 1 ribbing for Button and Buttonhole Bands and bottom ribbing
Alternate knit 1, purl 1.

4 × 2 ribbing for Body and Sleeves
Alternate knit 4, purl 2.

SELVEDGE STITCHES

On the Collar as well as the Button and Buttonhole Bands, all selvedge stitches at the beginning of every row are slipped purlwise with yarn in front of work and the selvedge stitches at the end of every row are knitted, to create a chained selvedge.

CONSTRUCTION NOTES

The sweater is worked seamlessly in one piece from the top down. Work begins at the Mock Turtleneck Collar from a magic cast-on. While the stitches on the 2nd needle are resting, the stitches on the 1st needle are used to work the double-layered mock turtleneck Collar in 2 × 2 ribbing. When the indicated height has been reached, the Collar is folded and the live stitches are knit together with the previously held stitches from the 2nd needle. Neckline shaping with short rows begins before regular raglan increases are worked in turned rows. After having completed the raglan increases, all stitches are placed on hold to work the Button Band. Stitches for the top placket of the Button Band are picked up along the front edge and worked in 1 × 1 ribbing. This is repeated at the opposite edge to create the under placket of the Button Band.
After this, the top placket is placed on top of the under placket, and stitches are picked up and knit from the bottom edges of the plackets to join work into the round. Then the Body is finished in the round. The Sleeves are likewise completed separately in the round. Finally, the ribbing at the bottom edge of Body and the Sleeve cuffs is worked in 1 × 1 ribbing.

Ribbed Sweater with Button-neck Collar

RELAXED FIT

LET'S START

Mock Turtleneck Collar

Using 2 circular needles in size US 6 (4.0 mm), 24 in (60 cm) long, and magic cast-on (page 10), cast on a total of 208/208/232/244/244/280/280 sts, or 104/104/116/122/122/140/140 sts onto each needle. The stitches on the back needle are immediately placed on hold and not worked at the present time.

Over the 104/104/116/122/122/140/140 sts of the front needle, work the Collar in turned rows in 2 × 2 ribbing. Work **Row 1 (RS row)** as follows: Selv st, [k2, p2] to last 3 sts, k2, selv st.

For the Collar, work 7.5/7.5/8/8/8.25/8.25/8.75 in (19/19/20/20/21/21/22 cm) in 2 × 2 ribbing, working all sts as they appear (knitting the knits and purling the purls), ending with a WS row.

Now the Collar will be closed up. Weave in all loose ends on the wrong side. Fold the Collar to the inside of the garment with the right side of the fabric facing outward. Take up the formerly held stitches, holding this needle in the back, and hold the needle bearing the stitches just used to work the Collar in front.

Work the 1st 7 sts of the front needle as they appear. Then transfer the 1st 7 sts of the back needle to a stitch holder or safety pin for holding. These 7 sts will later be turned into the inner facing of the Button Band. Then knit the following 90/90/102/108/108/126/126 sts of the front needle together with the 90/90/102/108/108/126/126 sts of the back needle. For this, slip each stitch from the back needle individually to the front needle and either knit or purl it together with the corresponding stitch on the front needle, depending on how the stitch appears (k2tog for knit sts and p2tog for purl sts).

Now 7 sts each remain on the front and on the back needle. Transfer the 7 sts of the back needle to a stitch holder or safety pin for holding. Work the 7 sts of the front needle as they appear (knitting the knits and purling the purls).

Dividing the Yoke and working short rows

In the following WS row, the 4 × 2 ribbing pattern for the Yoke will be set up. Place 8 markers as follows: Selv st, p2, work [k2, p4] 1/1/2/2/2/3/3 time(s) in all, k2 (Front), place m, p4 (raglan sts), place m, work [k2, p4] 2 times, k2 (Sleeve), place m, p4 (raglan sts), place m, work [k2, p4] 6/6/6/7/7/8/8 times in all, k2 (Back), place m, p4 (raglan sts), place m, work [k2, p4] 2 times, k2 (Sleeve), place m, p4 (raglan sts), place m, k2, work [p4, k2] 1/1/2/2/2/3/3 time(s) in all, p2, selv st (Front). The 4 × 2 ribbing pattern has now been set up, which makes starting the Yoke much easier, since from here on, all stitches are worked as they appear (knitting the knits and purling the purls).

Change to US 7 (4.5 mm) needles. You will now begin to work wrap and turn short rows (pages 14–15) and, at the same time, raglan increases.

Raglan increases will be worked from here on in every other row, always in a RS row, immediately to the right of (before) and to the left of (after) the column of 4 raglan stitches. To the right of (before) the raglan sts, always increase 1 st right-leaning from the bar between sts, to the left of (after) the raglan sts, always increase 1 st left-leaning from the bar between sts.

Incorporate the increased stitches into the 4 × 2 ribbing pattern as follows: Next to each column of 4 raglan stitches, there are currently 2 purl stitches. This means that the 1st 4 increases will be knit. The 5th and 6th increases will be purled before the sequence starts anew.

Row 1 (RS): Work sts as they appear (knitting the knits and purling the purls) to marker (Front), M1R from the bar between sts, slip m, k4 (raglan sts), slip m, M1L from the bar between sts, work sts to marker (Sleeve) as they appear, M1R from the bar between sts, slip m, k4 (raglan sts), slip m, M1L from the bar between sts, work sts to marker (Back) as they appear, M1R from the bar between sts, slip m, k4 (raglan sts), slip m, M1L from the bar between sts, work sts to marker (Sleeve) as they appear, M1R from the bar between sts, slip m, k4 (raglan sts), slip m, M1L from the bar between sts, work 2 sts as they appear, turn work.

Row 2 (WS): Work sts as they appear (knitting the knits and purling the purls) to marker (Front), slip m, p4 (raglan sts), slip m, work sts to marker (Sleeve) as they appear, slip m, p4 (raglan sts), slip m, work sts to marker (Back) as they appear, slip m, p4 (raglan sts), slip m, work sts to marker (Sleeve) as they appear, slip m, p4 (raglan sts), slip m, 2 sts as they appear, turn work.

Repeat Rows 1 and 2 another 2/2/3/3/3/4/4 times, always working 3 sts past the previous turning spot.

Work a RS row with increases over the remaining sts of the row, to finish off the short row section:

RS Row: Work sts as they appear (knitting the knits and purling the purls) to marker (Front), M1R from the bar between sts, slip m, k4 (raglan sts), slip m, M1L from the bar between sts, work sts to marker (Sleeve) as they appear, M1R from the bar between sts, slip m, k4 (raglan sts), slip m, M1L from the bar between sts, work sts to marker (Back) as they appear, M1R from the bar between sts, slip m, k4 (raglan sts), slip m, M1L from the bar between sts, work sts to marker (Sleeve) as they appear, M1R from the bar between sts, slip m, k4 (raglan sts), slip m, M1L from the bar between sts, work all remaining sts of the row (Front) as they appear, selv st.

WS Row (without increases): Work all sts as they appear (knitting the knits and purling the purls), slipping all markers as you encounter them.

While working the short row section, you have already completed the 1st 4/4/5/5/5/6/6 raglan increases.

Please note: Raglan increases #5 and #6 need to be purled in order to fit correctly into the 4 × 2 ribbing pattern!

There are 136/136/156/162/162/188/188 sts on the needles: 4 raglan sts each, 15/15/22/22/22/29/29 sts for each Front, 22/22/24/24/24/26/26 sts for each Sleeve, and 46/46/48/54/54/62/62 sts for the Back.

Yoke

Work the following 2 rows a total of 14/14/19/19/19/18/24 times:

Row 1 (RS): Work sts as they appear (knitting the knits and purling the purls) to marker (Front), M1R from the bar between sts, slip m, k4 (raglan sts), slip m, M1L from the bar between sts, work sts to marker (Sleeve) as they appear, M1R from the bar between sts, slip m, k4 (raglan sts), slip m, M1L from the bar between sts, work sts to marker (Back) as they appear, M1R from the bar between sts, slip m, k4 (raglan sts), slip m, M1L from the bar between sts, work sts to marker (Sleeve) as they appear, M1R from the bar between sts, slip m, k4 (raglan sts), slip m, M1L from the bar between sts, work all remaining sts of the row (Front) as they appear.

Row 2 (WS): Work all sts as they appear (knitting the knits and purling the purls), slipping all markers as you encounter them.

You have now completed a total of 18/18/24/24/24/24/30 raglan increases.

There are 248/248/308/314/314/332/380 sts on the needles: 4 raglan sts each, 29/29/41/41/41/47/53 sts for each Front, 50/50/62/62/62/62/74 sts for each Sleeve, and 74/74/86/92/92/98/110 sts for the Back. Transfer all sts to a spare needle, extra cord, or piece of waste yarn for holding.

ARE YOU MAKING THIS SWEATER FOR A MAN OR WOMAN?

For a woman's garment, the Right Front is closed over the Left Front. The Button Band on the Right Front is the top placket—on this placket, the 4 buttonholes will be worked. The Button Band on the Left Front is the under placket—to this placket, the 4 buttons will be attached.

For a man's garment, the Left Front is closed over the Right Front. The Button Band on the Left Front is the top placket—on this placket, the 4 buttonholes will be worked. The Button Band on the Right Front is the under placket—to this placket, the 4 buttons will be attached.

Button and Buttonhole Bands

You will now pick up and knit stitches along the front edges.

For the Button Band on Left Front, begin picking up along the bottom edge (at the previously held stitches) and end at the top at the Collar. For the Button Band on Right Front, begin at the top along the fold line of the Collar, and end at the bottom at the previously held stitches.

Pick up a total of 59/59/71/71/71/71/83 sts along the front edge at a ratio of 8 sts picked up from every 9 sts (picking up 1 st from each of 8 consecutive sts and skipping the 9th st), if picking up a different number, make sure to pick up an odd number of stitches.

Button Band without buttonholes

Row 1 is a WS row. Set up the 1 × 1 ribbing pattern as follows: Selv st, [p1, k1] to last 2 sts, p1, selv st. Work 14 rows in 1 × 1 ribbing, working all sts as they appear (knitting the knits and purling the purls). Bind off all sts using the Italian bind-off method (page 29).

Buttonhole Band with buttonholes

Row 1 is a WS row. Set up the 1 × 1 ribbing pattern as follows: Selv st, [p1, k1] to last 2 sts, p1, selv st. Work 6 rows in 1 × 1 ribbing, working all sts as they appear (knitting the knits and purling the purls). Then, work the buttonholes as follows: Selv st, work 6/6/6/6/6/6/9 sts in ribbing pattern, BO 3 sts, work 11/11/

15/15/15/15/17 sts in ribbing pattern, BO 3 sts, work 11/11/15/15/15/15/17 sts in ribbing pattern, BO 3 sts, work 11/11/15/15/15/15/17 sts in ribbing pattern, BO 3 sts, work 6/6/6/6/6/6/9 sts in ribbing pattern, selv st. Work 1 WS row, working all sts as they appear (knitting the knits and purling the purls). Atop each bound-off buttonhole, cast on 3 new sts.

Work 6 rows, working all sts as they appear. Bind off all sts using the Italian bind-off method (page 29). Now place the appropriate top placket of the Button Band on top of the under placket. Join new working yarn and, using the right needle tip bearing the previously held Yoke stitches, pick up and knit 10 sts along the bottom edge of the Button Band. This has joined work into the round.

Body

In the next step, the Sleeve stitches will be placed on hold. Raglan stitches are reallocated to the Body, and the marker for the BoR is placed in a new spot. Work all sts to marker as they appear, remove m, k4, slip marker. From here on, this marker will be the new BoR! Place the following 50/50/62/62/62/62/74 sts on hold, cast on 8/14/2/2/8/8/8 new sts, remove m, k4, remove m, work 74/74/86/92/92/98/110 sts as they appear, remove m, k4, remove m, place the following 50/50/62/62/62/62/74 sts on hold, cast on 8/14/2/2/8/8/8 new sts, remove m, k4, remove m, work all sts to the new marker for the BoR as they appear.
There are 174/186/198/204/216/234/258 sts on the needles.

Please note: The newly cast-on sts in the center front will be worked as k1, p2, k4, p2, k1, the former selv sts of the front edge will be knit. This completes the pattern repeat of the 4 × 2 ribbing in the center front. The newly cast-on underarm stitches, too, will be integrated into the 4 × 2 ribbing pattern as listed for each size: p2, k4, p2/[p2, k4] twice, p2/p2/p2/p2, k4, p2/p2, k4, p2/p2, k4, p2.

Work in the round, all sts as they appear (knitting the knits and purling the purls), until the sweater measures approximately 17.25/17.75/18/18.5/19/19.25/19.75 in (44/45/46/47/48/49/50 cm) from the transition between Collar and Yoke. Change to US 6 (4.0 mm) needles and work 2.25 in (6 cm) in 1 × 1 ribbing. Bind off all sts using the Italian bind-off method (page 29).

Sleeves

Place the 50/50/62/62/62/62/74 sts of the 1st Sleeve onto a circular needle in size US 7 (4.5 mm), 16 in (40 cm) long, and pick up and knit 10/16/4/10/16/16/10 sts from the newly cast-on underarm stitches at the side of the Body. There are 60/66/66/72/78/78/84 sts on the needles.
Since the pattern repeat at the underside of the Sleeve is different from that at the side of the Body, the number of stitches picked up at the side of the Body does not match the number of stitches picked up at the Sleeve.
If you have noticeably more stitches at the Sleeve than at the Body, you can pick up new stitches from the stitches at the transition between Front or Back and

Sleeve. Place a marker for the BoR after the 1st 5/8/2/5/8/8/5 of the 10/16/4/10/16/16/10 sts.

Work the newly cast-on Sleeve sts as follows: k4, p2, k4/[k4, p2] twice, k4/k4/k4, p2, k4/[k4, p2] twice, k4/[k4, p2] twice, k4/k4, p2, k4.
Work in 4 × 2 ribbing pattern in the round, all sts as they appear. At the same time, work decreases on the underside of the Sleeve in every 16th/14th/14th/10th/10th/12th/10th round a total of 5/6/6/8/8/7/8 times.

Work **decrease round** as follows:
Sizes 1, 4, and 7: Ssp, work all sts as they appear to last 3 sts, p2tog.
Sizes 2, 3, 5, and 6: K1, ssk, work all sts as they appear to last 3 sts, k2tog, k1.
After having completed 5/6/6/8/8/7/8 decreases, a total of 80/84/84/80/80/84/80 rounds have been worked. The Sleeve has now reached a length of 12.25/12.5/12.5/12.25/12.25/12.5/12.25 in (31/32/32/31/31/32/31 cm). There are 50/54/54/56/62/64/68 sts on the needles. Continue to work in the round, all sts as they appear, until the Sleeve measures 15/15.25/15.75/16.25/16.5/17/17.25 in (38/39/40/41/42/43/44 cm) from the underarm. At this point, the Sleeve can be lengthened or shortened according to your personal preferences. Change to US 6 (4.0 mm) needles and work 2.25 in (6 cm) in 1 × 1 ribbing. Bind off all stitches.
Work the 2nd Sleeve the same way.

Finishing
First, place the 7 previously held stitches on the inside of the right Collar onto a US 6 (4.0 mm) DPN. Join

new working yarn and work the following 2 rows 16/16/22/22/22/22/28 times:
Row 1 (RS): Selv st, k5, selv st.
Row 2 (WS): Selv st, p5, selv st.
Transfer these 7 sts to a stitch holder or safety pin for holding.
Then place the 7 previously held stitches on the inside of the left Collar onto a US 6 (4.0 mm) DPN. Join new working yarn and here, too, work the following 2 rows 16/16/22/22/22/22/28 times:
Row 1 (RS): Selv st, k5, selv st.
Row 2 (WS): Selv st, p5, selv st.
In the next RS row, join the left and right facing as follows: Selv st, k6, cast on 7 new sts. Take up the previously held stitches of the other facing strip, and work k6, selv st.
Work another 1.25 in (3 cm) in stockinette stitch in turned rows, then bind off all stitches.
Using a sewing needle and sewing thread in a matching color to make small stitches to create a smooth and straight finish, sew both facing strips over the cast-on edge of the Button Band.

Weave in all ends and wash the sweater in lukewarm water with a mild wool detergent. Block it spread out flat on an even, horizontal surface, and let it dry. Sew the buttons to the Button Band at the level of the buttonholes on the opposite Buttonhole Band.

Riley

This hoodie in a textured pattern will keep your head warm on colder days. Casually combined with jeans and sneakers, it is a fashion winner!

MATERIALS

· Lamana Como Grande; bulky weight; 100% pure new wool; 131 yds (120 m) per 1.75 oz (50 g); in 46 Basalt Blue: 9/10/11/13/15/17/18 skeins
  Total yardage required: 1,181/1,312/1,444/1,706/ 1,968.5/2,231/2,3620 yds (1,080/1,200/1,320/ 1,560/1,800/2,040/2,160 m)
· Circular knitting needles in size US 8 (5.0 mm), 16 in (40 cm), 24 in (60 cm), 32 in (80 cm), and 40/ 48 in (100/120 cm) long
· Circular knitting needle in size US 6 (4.0 mm), 32 in (80 cm) long
· DPN sets in US 6 (4.0 mm) and US 8 (5.0 mm)
· Tapestry needle for weaving in ends
· Stitch markers

SIZES

1/2/3/4/5/6/7
Incorporated positive ease: 3.25–4.75 in (8–12 cm)
Chest circumference: 36.25/38.5/41/43.75/46.5/49.25/ 53.25 in (92/98/104/111/118/125/135 cm)
Upper arm circumference: 12.5/13.75/14.25/15.75/ 16.5/18.5/20.5 in (32/35/36.5/40/42.5/47/52 cm)
Length: 22/22.75/23.5/23.5/24.5/25.25/26 in (56/58/ 60/60/62/64/66 cm)
Our model wears size 3 (Women's M / Men's S)

GAUGE

17 sts and 26 rows = 4 × 4 in (10 × 10 cm) in Textured Pattern on US 8 (5.0 mm) needles (after washing and blocking)

STITCH PATTERNS

Textured Pattern in turned rows
The Textured Pattern has a pattern repeat of 4 sts widthwise and 8 rows heightwise.
Row 1 (RS): Knit all stitches.
Row 2 (WS): Purl all stitches.
Row 3 (RS): *K1-tbl, p1, rep from * to end of row.
Row 4 (WS): *K1, p1-tbl, rep from * to end of row.
Row 5 (RS): Work as Row 1.
Row 6 (WS): Work as Row 2.
Row 7 (RS): *P1, k1-tbl, rep from * to end of row.
Row 8 (WS): *P1-tbl, k1, rep from * to end of row.

Textured Pattern in the round
The Textured Pattern has a pattern repeat of 4 sts widthwise and 8 rounds heightwise.
Rnds 1–2: Knit all stitches.
Rnds 3–4: *K1-tbl, p1, rep from * around.
Rnds 5–6: Work as Rounds 1–2.
Rnds 7–8: *P1, k1-tbl, rep from * around.

Ribbing
Alternate knit 1, purl 1.

Selvedge stitches
All selvedge stitches in all rows are always knitted.

CONSTRUCTION NOTES

The hood is worked first, beginning at the top of the head, then the sides of the hood are worked in turned rows. Along the front edge, you then work the hood's ribbing before work is joined into the round. After completing the Yoke in a Textured Pattern with traditional raglan increases, the Sleeves are placed on hold. Body and Sleeves are then finished separately in the same Textured Pattern.

126

REGULAR FIT

LET'S START

Top of Head
Using circular needle in size US 8 (5.0 mm), 24 in (60 cm) long, cast on a total of 29/29/31/31/35/35/37 sts.
Row 1 (WS): Purl all stitches.
Begin working Textured Pattern in turned rows as follows:
Row 1 (RS): Selv st, knit to last stitch, selv st.
Row 2 (WS): Selv st, purl to last stitch, selv st.
Row 3 (RS): Selv st, [k1-tbl, p1] 13/13/14/14/16/16/17 times, k1-tbl, selv st.
Row 4 (WS): Selv st, p1-tbl, [k1, p1-tbl] 13/13/14/14/16/16/17 times, selv st.
Row 5 (RS): Work as Row 1.
Row 6 (WS): Work as Row 2.
Row 7 (RS): Selv st, [p1, k1-tbl] 13/13/14/14/16/16/17 times, p1, selv st.
Row 8 (WS): Selv st, k1, [p1-tbl, k1] to last st, selv st.

You have now completed the 1st 8 rows and thus worked a full repeat of the Textured Pattern. At the left edge of the knitted piece, the pattern repeat is incomplete, there is just 1 stitch of it so far. This will result in the stitch pattern at the top of the head turning out symmetrical. Now repeat the 8 rows described above continuously until work measures 4.75/4.75/6/6/6/6/7 in (12/12/15/15/15/15/18 cm) from cast-on edge, ending this part with a WS row and a Row 8 of the pattern repeat. Break the working yarn.

Side of Head
Join new working yarn and, starting at the right side edge of the top of the head, pick up and knit a total of 30/30/34/34/34/34/38 sts. Now knit all sts at the top of the head. After this, pick up and knit a total of 30/30/34/34/34/34/38 sts along the left side edge of the top of the head the same way. You now have a total of 89/89/99/99/103/103/113 sts on the needles and will work over all stitches in Textured Pattern as before, in turned rows.

The following row is a WS row, Row 2 of the pattern repeat:
Row 2 (WS): Selv st, purl to last stitch, selv st.
Row 3 (RS): Selv st, [k1-tbl, p1] to last 2 sts, k1-tbl, selv st.
Row 4 (WS): Selv st, p1-tbl, [k1, p1-tbl to last st, selv st.

Row 5 (RS): Selv st, knit to last stitch, selv st.
Row 6 (WS): Work as Row 2.
Row 7 (RS): Selv st, [p1, k1-tbl to last 2 sts, p1, selv st.
Row 8 (WS): Selv st, k1, [p1-tbl, k1] to last st, selv st.

Repeat the 8 rows described above according to the pattern repeat until the sides of the hood have reached a length of 8.25/9.5/9.5/9.5/9.5/9.5/10.5/10.5 in (21/24/24/24/24/24/27/27 cm) measured from cast-on edge, ending with a WS row and with a Row 8 of the pattern repeat. Now it's time to begin the Nape decreases.

Nape Decreases
Decreases are located at the nape side to reduce bulkiness in the center Back of the hood. This makes the hood drape better. Decreases are worked in every other row (always in a RS row) a total of 6/6/10/10/8/8/12 times.
In the following row, you will place 2 markers, while working the 1st 2 decreases at the same time:
RS Row: Selv st, k37/37/41/41/43/43/47, k2tog, place m, k9/9/11/11/11/11/13, place m, skp, k37/37/41/41/43/43/47, selv st.
WS Row: Selv st, purl to last stitch, selv st.
You have now placed 2 markers and already decreased 2 sts. All further decreases are from here on always worked immediately before the 1st marker and after the 2nd marker. Before the 1st marker, a right-leaning decrease is worked, after the 2nd marker, a left-leaning decrease is worked.

Depending on which spot of the pattern is to be worked, incorporate the decreases into the stitch pattern as follows:
If the last stitch before the marker is a knit stitch (or k-tbl), work k2tog (= right-leaning).
If the last stitch before the marker is a purl stitch, work p2tog (= right-leaning).
If the 1st stitch after the marker is a knit stitch (or k-tbl), work skp (= left-leaning).
If the 1st stitch after the marker is a purl stitch, work ssp (= left-leaning).

Work the following 2 rows 5/5/9/9/7/7/11 times:
RS Row: Selv st, work the Textured Pattern according to the pattern repeat to 2 sts before the 1st marker, 1 dec, slip m, work 9/9/11/11/11/11/13 sts to next marker

128

according to the pattern repeat for the Textured Pattern, slip m, 1 dec, work to last stitch according to the pattern repeat for the Textured Pattern, selv st.

WS Row: Selv st, work the Textured Pattern according to the pattern repeat, slipping all markers as you encounter them, selv st.

You have now worked a total of 6/6/10/10/8/8/12 decrease rows, during which you have decreased 12/12/20/20/16/16/24 sts in all. Remove both markers. All nape decreases have been completed.

You have a total of 77/77/79/79/87/87/89 sts on the needles. Break the working yarn and set these stitches temporarily aside on a spare needle or cord.

Hood Ribbing

Using a circular needle in size US 6 (4.0 mm), 32 in (80 cm) long, pick up stitches for the hood's ribbing along the front edge.

Start at the bottom edge of the right side of the head and work your way upward in the direction of the top of head. Along the side of the head, pick up from the selvedge stitches of the knotted selvedge at a rate of 8 sts from every 9 sts. This means that you will pick up 1 st each from 8 consecutive sts and skip the 9th stitch (for a total of 50/56/56/56/56/64/64 sts).

Along the top of head, pick up 1 stitch from every stitch of the cast-on row (for a total of 27/27/29/29/33/33/35 sts).

Proceed by picking up along the edge on the left side of the head, again at a rate of 8 sts from every 9 sts (for a total of 50/56/56/56/56/64/64 sts).

You now have a total of 127/139/141/141/145/161/163 sts on the needles for the hood's ribbing.

Row 1 is a WS row. Set up the ribbing as follows: Selv st, [p1, k1] to last 2 sts, p1, selv st.

Work 4/4/6/6/6/6/8 more rows in ribbing, beginning with a RS row, and working all sts as they appear (knitting the knits and purling the purls).

Now it's time to work short row shaping for the hood's ribbing:

RS Row: Selv st, 48 sts in ribbing pattern; turn work.
WS Row: Work in ribbing pattern to last st, selv st.
RS Row: Selv st, 36 sts in ribbing pattern; turn work.
WS Row: Work in ribbing pattern to last st, selv st.
RS Row: Selv st, 24 sts in ribbing pattern; turn work.
WS Row: Work in ribbing pattern to last st, selv st.
RS Row: Selv st, 12 sts in ribbing pattern; turn work.
WS Row: Work in ribbing pattern to last st, selv st.

Work a complete RS row over all stitches in ribbing pattern, working all sts as they appear (knitting the knits and purling the purls).

WS Row: Selv st, 48 sts in ribbing pattern; turn work.
RS Row: Work in ribbing pattern to last st, selv st.
WS Row: Selv st, 36 sts in ribbing pattern; turn work.
RS Row: Work in ribbing pattern to last st, selv st.
WS Row: Selv st, 24 sts in ribbing pattern; turn work.
RS Row: Work in ribbing pattern to last st, selv st.
WS Row: Selv st, 12 sts in ribbing pattern; turn work.
RS Row: Work in ribbing pattern to last st, selv st.

Work a complete WS row over all stitches in ribbing pattern, working all sts as they appear. Short row shaping on the hood's ribbing has now been completed.

Beginning with a RS row, work 4/4/4/4/4/4/4 more rows in ribbing pattern, working all sts as they appear. Bind off all sts using the Italian bind-off method (page 29).

Yoke

Join work into the round and begin working the Yoke. For this, place the bottom edges of the hood's ribbing atop each other as described below.

ARE YOU MAKING THIS SWEATER FOR A MAN OR WOMAN?

For a woman's garment, the Right Front is closed over the Left Front. The right half of the ribbing is the top placket, the left half of the ribbing is the under placket. For a man's garment, the Left Front is closed over the Right Front. The left half of the ribbing is the top placket, the right half of the ribbing is the under placket.

Join new working yarn and, using the tip of the right needle (still bearing the 77/77/79/79/87/87/89 sts of the hood), pick up and knit a total of 7/7/9/9/9/9/11 sts from the bottom edges of the hood. By this, you have joined work into the round. You now have a combined 84/84/88/88/96/96/100 sts on the needles. Continue working in the round, and please note that this slightly changes the pattern repeat of the Textured Pattern!

In the next step, you will mark the BoR: k10/10/10/10/11/11/10, place a marker onto the left needle. The marker just placed is the new BoR.

You will now begin to work raglan increases. In preparation for this, in the following round (Round 1 of the pattern repeat for the Textured Pattern), place stitch markers for the increase spots and, at the same time, work the 1st increase round:

Rnd 1: M1R from the bar between sts, slip BoR marker, k1, p1, k1 (raglan sts), place m, M1L from the bar between sts, k9/9/9/9/9/11/13 (Sleeve sts), M1R from the bar between sts, place m, k1, p1, k1 (raglan sts), place m, M1L from the bar between sts, k27/27/29/29/31/31/31 (Back), M1R from the bar between sts, place m, k1, p1, k1 (raglan sts), place m, M1L from the bar between sts, k9/9/9/9/9/11/13 (Sleeve sts), M1R from the bar between sts, place m, k1, p1, k1 (raglan sts), place m, M1L from the bar between sts, knit to BoR marker (Front).

Rnd 2: Slip BoR marker, k1, p1, k1 (raglan sts), slip m, knit to next m (Sleeve), slip m, k1, p1, k1 (raglan sts), slip m, knit to next m, slip m, k1, p1, k1 (raglan sts), slip m, knit to next m, slip m, k1, p1, k1 (raglan sts), slip m, knit to BoR marker.

You have now increased a total of 8 sts and divided the knitted piece into sections with markers. From here on, increases will be worked in every other round immediately before and after the respective 3 raglan sts: before (to the right of) the column of raglan sts, M1R from the bar between sts; after (to the left of) the column of raglan sts, M1L from the bar between sts.

Please note: Depending on the current round of the pattern repeat, the increased stitch will either be knitted or purled. From the very beginning, the increased stitches need to be incorporated into the stitch pattern for the Front, Back, and Sleeves of the garment.

Work the following 2 rounds a total of 19/23/23/28/28/32/36 times:

Rnd 1: M1R from the bar between sts, slip BoR marker, k1, p1, k1 (raglan sts), slip m, M1L from the bar between sts, work all sts to next marker (Sleeve) following the appropriate round of the pattern repeat, M1R from the bar between sts, place m, k1, p1, k1 (raglan sts), place m, M1L from the bar between sts, work all sts to next marker (Back) following the appropriate round of the pattern repeat, M1R from the bar between sts, place m, k1, p1, k1 (raglan sts), place m, M1L from the bar between sts, work all sts to next marker (Sleeve) following the appropriate round of

the pattern repeat, M1R from the bar between sts, place m, k1, p1, k1 (raglan sts), place m, M1L from the bar between sts, work all sts to BoR marker following the appropriate round of the pattern repeat.

Rnd 2: Slip BoR marker, k1, p1, k1 (raglan sts), slip m, knit to next m (Sleeve), slip m, k1, p1, k1 (raglan sts), slip m, knit to next m (Back), slip m, k1, p1, k1 (raglan sts), slip m, knit to next m (Sleeve), slip m, k1, p1, k1 (raglan sts), slip m, knit to BoR marker (Front). You have now worked 20/24/24/28/28/32/36 raglan increases and, during this, increased a total of 160/192/192/224/224/256/288 sts. The last round to be worked is a Round 8 of the pattern repeat.

You have a total of 244/276/280/312/316/352/388 sts on the needles. Divide the sts into sections as follows:

Front and Back: 67/75/77/85/87/95/103 sts each; raglan stitch columns: 3 sts each; Sleeves: 49/57/57/65/65/75/85 sts each.

The Yoke has now been finished. In the next step, the Sleeve stitches will be placed on hold and the former raglan sts will be reallocated to the Body.

Body

Slip BoR marker, k1, p1, k1, remove m, transfer the following 49/57/57/65/65/75/85 sts (Sleeve) to a stitch holder or piece of waste yarn, cast on 5/3/5/3/7/5/5 new underarm sts, remove m, k1, p1, k1, remove m, k67/75/77/85/87/95/103 (Row 1 of the pattern repeat on the Back), remove m, k1, p1, k1, remove m, transfer the following 49/57/57/65/65/75/85 sts (Sleeve) to a stitch holder or piece of waste yarn, cast on 5/3/5/3/7/5/5 new underarm sts, remove m, k1, p1, k1, remove m, k the following 67/75/77/85/87/95/103 sts (Row 1 of the pattern repeat on the Front). The only marker still remaining is the marker for the BoR.

You now have a total of 156/168/176/188/200/212/228 sts for the Body on the needles. The Sleeve stitches will be held for later.

Continue to work the pattern repeat for the Textured Pattern, continuously repeating Rounds 1–8 (now, beginning with a Round 2).

The newly cast-on underarm sts and the raglan sts will be incorporated into the stitch pattern of the Front and Back and will likewise be worked in Textured Pattern from here on.

Work in Textured Pattern in the round until the Body measures 13.5/13/13.75/12.5/13.5/13/12.5 in (34/33/

Work the Sleeve in Textured Pattern in the round, at the same time working Sleeve tapering decreases as described below at the underside of the Sleeve in every 12th/10th/10th/8th/8th/7th/6th rnd, a total of 6/8/8/10/10/12/16 times.

Work **decrease round** as follows: Work 1 st in stitch pattern per pattern repeat, either k2tog or p2tog, work in stitch pattern per pattern repeat to last 3 sts of the round, either ssk or ssp (depending on the current round of the pattern repeat), work 1 st in stitch pattern per pattern repeat.

After having completed the 6th/8th/8th/10th/10th/12th/16th decrease round, you have decreased a total of 12/16/16/20/20/24/32 sts. 42/44/46/48/52/56/58 sts remain on the needles.

Work in Textured Pattern in the round until the Sleeve has reached a length of 13.25/13.75/14.25/14.5/15/15.25/15.75 in (34/35/36/37/38/39/40 cm), measured from the underarm. At this point, the Sleeve can be lengthened or shortened according to your personal preferences. Change to US 6 (4.0 mm) DPN set and work 2.25 in (6.0 cm) in 1 × 1 ribbing pattern. Bind off all sts using the Italian bind-off method (page 29). Work the 2nd Sleeve the same way.

Finishing
Weave in all ends and wash the hoodie in lukewarm water with a mild wool detergent. Block it spread out flat on an even, horizontal surface, and let it dry.

35/32/34/33/32 cm) from the armhole. At this point, the overall length of the Hoodie can be adjusted according to your personal preferences. Change to circular needle in size US 6 (4.0 mm), 32 in (80 cm), and work 2.4 in (6.0 cm) in 1 × 1 ribbing pattern. Bind off all sts using the Italian bind-off method (page 29).

Sleeves
Place the 49/57/57/65/65/75/85 sts of the 1st Sleeve onto a circular needle in size US 8 (5.0 mm), 16 in (40 cm) long. Pick up and knit a total of 5/3/5/3/7/5/5 sts from the newly cast-on underarm sts at the side of the Body. Join to work in the round. After the 1st 3 of the newly cast-on sts, place a marker for the BoR. You now have a total of 54/60/62/68/72/80/90 sts on the needles.

Alex

This zippered sweater is my personal favorite! Its textured stitch pattern and tall stand-up collar with zipper coupled with the robust yarn are the perfect combination for me.

MATERIALS
· 2 strands Lamana Shetland; fingering weight; 100% pure new wool; 153 yds (140 m) per 0.9 oz (25 g); in 25 Copper: 8/8/9/10/10/12/13 skeins *held together with*
1 strand Lang Yarns Jawoll; sock weight; 75% pure new wool, 25% polyamide/nylon; 230 yds (210 m) per 1.75 oz (50 g); in 83.0215 Nougat: 5/6/6/7/7/8/9 skeins
Total yardage required: 1,094/1,203/1,312/1,422/1,531/1,750/1,968.5 yds (1,000/1,100/1,200/1,300/1,400/1,600/1,800 m)
· Circular knitting needles in size US 8 (5.0 mm), 16 in (40 cm), 24 in (60 cm), 32 in (80 cm), and 40/48 in (100/120 cm) long
· Circular knitting needles in size US 6 (4.0 mm), 16 in (40 cm), 2 each in 24 in (60 cm), 32 in (80 cm), and 48 in (120 cm) long
· DPN sets in sizes US 6 (4.0 mm) and US 8 (5.0 mm)
· 1 zipper, 11 in (28 cm) long, and sewing thread in a matching color
· Tapestry needle for weaving in ends
· Stitch markers
· 2 safety pins

SIZES
1/2/3/4/5/6/7
Incorporated positive ease: 8–13.75 in (20–35 cm)
Chest circumference: 43.25/46/49.25/52/54.75/57.5/60.25 in (110/117/125/132/139/146/153 cm)
Upper arm circumference: 12.25/13/14.25/15/16.5/17.25/18 in (31/33/36/38/42/44/46 cm)
Length: 20.5/21/21.25/21.75/22/22.5/22.75 in (52/53/54/55/56/57/58 cm)
Our model wears size 4 (Women's L / Men's M)

GAUGE
17 sts and 26 rows = 4 × 4 in (10 × 10 cm) in stockinette stitch with 3 strands of yarn held together on US 8 (5.0 mm) needles (after washing and blocking)

STITCH PATTERNS
1 × 1 ribbing for Stand-up Collar and bottom edge
Alternate knit 1, purl 1.

Stockinette stitch in turned rows for the Sleeves
RS Rows: Knit all stitches.
WS Rows: Purl all sts.

Stockinette stitch in the round for the Sleeves
Knit all stitches.

Textured Pattern
Please refer to chart. The chart shows how the stitch pattern is set up during the Shoulder increases and can be continued over the whole Body the same way.

Selvedge Stitches
The selvedge stitch at the Collar/along the zipper side of the Yoke at the end of every row is always knitted. The selvedge stitch at the beginning of every row is slipped (purlwise) with yarn in front of work.

CONSTRUCTION NOTES
The double-layered Stand-up Collar is worked first, folded, and knit together. Then the Textured Pattern is set up according to the chart, while first Shoulder shaping then raglan increases are worked in turned rows. When the length of the opening for the zipper has been reached, work is joined into the round, the Yoke is finished, then the Sleeve stitches are placed on hold.
The Body is worked in Textured Pattern in the round, and the Sleeves are finished in stockinette stitch in the round.
Finally, the zipper is sewn into the garment and the interior facing along the zipper opening is added.
Work with 3 strands of yarn held together throughout.

Pullover with Zippered Stand-up Collar

**LOOSE FIT/
OVERSIZED**

LET'S START

Note: Work with 3 strands of yarn held together throughout.

Stand-up Collar

Using 2 circular needles in size US 6 (4.0 mm), 24 in (60 cm) long and magic cast-on (page 10), cast on a total of 182/182/182/182/206/206/206 sts, or 91/91/91/91/103/103/103 sts onto each needle. Immediately transfer the sts of the front needle to a stitch holder or piece of waste yarn for holding—they will not be worked at this time. Over the 91/91/91/91/103/103 sts of the back needle, work the Collar in 1 × 1 ribbing in turned rows.

Row 1 (RS): Selv st, [p1, k1] to last 2 sts, p1, selv st.
For the Collar, work 8 in (20 cm) in 1 × 1 ribbing, working all sts as they appear (knitting the knits and purling the purls), ending with a WS row.

The 2 layers of the Collar will be joined to close the Collar. First, weave in all loose ends on the wrong side of the Collar.

Fold the Collar to the inside of the garment with the right sides of the fabric facing outward. The formerly held sts are on the back needle. The sts over which you have just worked the Collar are on the front needle.

Work the 1st 7 sts of the front needle as they appear. Then transfer the 1st 7 sts of the back needle to a stitch holder or safety pin for holding. These 7 sts will later be turned into the inner facing for the zipper.

Now, either knit or purl the following 77/77/77/77/89/89/89 sts of the front needle together with the 77/77/77/77/89/89/89 sts of the back needle. To do this, slip the stitches from the back needle to the front needle 1 by 1, slipping 1 st from the back needle at a time, and either knitting or purling it together with the corresponding stitch of the front needle, depending on whether the stitch on the front needle is a knit or a purl stitch.

7 sts each remain on the front and on the back needle. Transfer the 7 sts of the back needle to a stitch holder or safety pin for holding. Work the 7 sts of the front needle as they appear.

Divide the Yoke and Work Shoulder Increases

The respective 3 Shoulder/raglan sts are set up as p1, k1, p1 and worked as they appear (knitting the knits and purling the purls) throughout.

Work a WS row over all stitches in 1 × 1 ribbing, placing 8 markers as follows:
Work 17/17/17/17/19/19/19 sts in 1 × 1 ribbing (Front), place m, work 3 sts in 1 × 1 ribbing (Shoulder/raglan sts), place m, work 5/5/5/5/7/7/7 sts in 1 × 1 ribbing (Sleeve), place m, work 3 sts in 1 × 1 ribbing (Shoulder/raglan sts), place m, work 35/35/35/35/39/39/39 sts in 1 × 1 ribbing (Back), place m, work 3 sts in 1 × 1 ribbing (Shoulder/raglan sts), place m, work 5/5/5/5/7/7/7 sts in 1 × 1 ribbing (Sleeve), place m, work 3 sts in 1 × 1 ribbing (Shoulder/raglan sts), work 17/17/17/17/19/19/19 sts in 1 × 1 ribbing (Front).

In the next (RS) row, begin to work the Shoulder increases. Shoulder increases are worked in every row (RS and WS rows) on the Front and Back, immediately next to the Shoulder stitches. To the left of the Shoulder stitch, work M1L from the bar between stitches. To the right of the Shoulder stitch, work M1R from the bar between stitches. Either knit or purl the increased stitches according to the chart. Additionally, the Textured Pattern will now be set up. I recommend placing an additional stitch marker onto the stitch in the center of the Back, which will make it easier to follow the stitch pattern without missing the change of direction.

Change to US 8 (5.0 mm) needles. Using the appropriate chart for your size, work Rows 1–9/11/13/15/15/17/19 with increases. The last increase is worked in a RS row.
There are now 127/135/143/151/163/171/179 sts on the needles: 26/28/30/32/34/36/38 sts for each Front, 5/5/5/5/7/7/7 sts for each Sleeve, 3 Shoulder/raglan sts each, and 53/57/61/65/69/73/77 sts for the Back.
Work a WS row over all sts as they appear (knitting the knits and purling the purls).

Now begin working the Sleeve increases. Increases will be worked in every other row, always in a RS row. Work the following 2 rows 6/7/8/9/10/11/12 times in all:
RS Row: Selv st, work all sts to marker (Front) according to the pattern repeat, slip m, work 3 sts as they appear, slip m, M1L from the bar between sts, knit to m, M1R from the bar between sts, slip m, work 3 sts as they appear, slip m, work all sts to marker (Back) according to the pattern repeat, slip m, work 3 sts as they appear, slip m, M1L from the bar between sts,

knit to m, M1R from the bar between sts, slip m, work 3 sts as they appear, slip m, work all sts to marker (Front) according to the pattern repeat, selv st.

WS Row: Work all sts as they appear. Continue the stitch pattern on the Front and Back, staying in pattern.

Sleeve increases have now been completed. There are 151/163/175/187/203/215/227 sts on the needles: 26/28/30/32/34/36/38 sts for each Front, 17/19/21/23/27/29/31 sts for each Sleeve, 3 Shoulder/raglan sts each, and 53/57/61/63/69/73/77 sts for the Back.

While working the raglan increases, in Row 45 of the Front, join work into the round. For this, cast on 1 new stitch in the center front, thus completing the pattern repeat in the center front, move the BoR to the beginning of the raglan line on the Left Front, then continue to work in the round. Raglan increases are worked in every other row, always in a RS row, a total of 15/16/17/18/19/20/21 times. Join into the round as indicated for the size worked at the 12th/10th/8th/6th/5th/3th/1st raglan increase.

Please note: During the raglan increases, new stitches are added at the armhole to the Front and Back. The increased stitches are incorporated into the stitch pattern by either knitting or purling them according to the established stitch pattern, which is extended toward the sides.

For raglan increases before joining into the round, work the following 2 rows a total of 11/9/7/5/4/2/0 times:

RS Row: Selv st, work all sts to marker (Front) according to the pattern repeat, M1R from the bar between sts, slip m, work 3 sts as they appear, slip m, M1L from the bar between sts, knit to m, M1R from the bar between sts, slip m, work 3 sts as they appear, slip m, M1R from the bar between sts, work all sts to marker (Back) according to the pattern repeat, M1L from the bar between sts, slip m, work 3 sts as they appear, slip m, M1L from the bar between sts, knit to m, M1R from the bar between sts, slip m, work 3 sts as they appear, slip m, M1L from the bar between sts, work all sts to marker (Front) according to the pattern repeat, selv st.

WS Row: Work all sts as they appear. Continue the stitch pattern on the Front and Back, staying in pattern.

After having completed a total of 11/9/7/5/4/2/0 raglan increases, join to work in the round.
There are 239/235/231/227/235/231/227 sts on the needles in all: 37/37/37/37/38/38/38 sts for each Front, 75/75/75/75/77/77/77 sts for the Back, 39/37/35/33/35/33/31 sts for each Sleeve, and 3 raglan sts each.

Join into the round as follows:
RS Row: Selv st, work all sts to marker (Front) according to the pattern repeat, M1R from the bar between sts, slip m, work 3 sts as they appear, slip m, M1L from the bar between sts, knit to m, M1R from the bar between sts, slip m, work 3 sts as they appear, slip m, M1R from the bar between sts, work all sts to marker (Back) according to the pattern repeat, M1L from the bar between sts, slip m, work 3 sts as they appear, slip m, M1L from the bar between sts, knit to m, M1R from the bar between sts, slip m, work 3 sts as they appear, slip m, M1L from the bar between sts, work all sts to end of needle (Front) according to the pattern repeat, cast on 1 new stitch, continue in stitch pattern in the same manner over the sts of the Left Front to marker.

This has joined work into the round. The stitch marker at which you have arrived now will be the new marker for the BoR. Over the just worked sts of the Left Front, you have now worked an additional "false" row in stitch pattern in order to move the BoR. This additional row will not be noticeable in the finished garment.

Work 1 round even over all stitches without increases. In this round, begin as usual, working the next round of the pattern repeat.

Work another 3/6/9/12/14/17/20 raglan increases in the round as follows:

Rnd 1: M1R from the bar between sts, slip BoR marker, work 3 sts as they appear, slip m, M1L from the bar between sts, knit to m, M1R from the bar between sts, slip m, work 3 sts as they appear, slip m, M1R from the bar between sts, work all sts to marker (Back) according to the pattern repeat, M1L from the bar between sts, slip m, work 3 sts as they appear, slip m, M1L from the bar between sts, knit to m, M1R from the bar between sts, slip m, work 3 sts as they appear, slip m, M1L from the bar between sts, work all sts to marker (Front) according to the pattern repeat to the end of round.

Rnd 2: Work all sts as they appear. Continue the stitch pattern on the Front and Back, staying in pattern.

All raglan increases have now been completed. You now have a total of 272/292/312/332/356/376/396 sts on the needles: 47/51/55/59/64/69/73 sts for each Sleeve, 3 Shoulder/raglan sts each, 83/89/95/101/107/113/119 sts each for the Front and Back.

Now the Sleeve stitches will be placed on hold and Shoulder/raglan sts reallocated to the Body.

Body

Slip BoR marker, work 3 sts as they appear, remove m, place 47/51/55/59/64/69/73 sts on hold, CO 5 new underarm sts, remove m, work 3 sts as they appear, slip m, work all sts of the Back in pattern as they appear, slip m, work 3 sts as they appear, remove m, place 47/51/55/59/64/69/73 sts on hold, CO 5 new underarm sts, remove m, work 3 sts as they appear, slip m, work all Front sts according to the charted pattern repeat to BoR marker.

There are 188/200/212/224/236/248/260 sts on the needles. The newly cast-on underarm stitches as well as the former Shoulder/raglan sts will be worked in 1 × 1 ribbing, the sts of the Front and Back as before

according to the pattern repeat of the established stitch pattern.

Work in the round until the Body has reached a length of 18/18.5/19/19.25/19.75/20/20.5 in (46/47/48/49/50/51/52 cm), measured from the Shoulder.

Change to US 6 (4.0 mm) needles and work 2.25 in (6 cm) in 1 × 1 ribbing, beginning with p1. Bind off all sts using the Italian bind-off method (page 29).

Sleeves

Place the 47/51/55/59/65/69/73 previously held sts of the 1st Sleeve onto a circular needle in size US 8 (5.0 mm), 16 in (40 cm) long, and pick up and knit 5 sts from the newly cast-on underarm stitches (= 52/56/

60/64/70/74/78 sts). Place a marker for the BoR after 3 of the 5 sts.

Now work stockinette stitch in the round, at the same time working Sleeve tapering decreases at the underside of the Sleeve in every 12th rnd, 6 times in all.

Work **Sleeve tapering decrease round** as follows: K1, ssk, k to last 3 sts, k2tog, k1.

After having completed 6 decreases, a total of 72 rounds have been worked. The Sleeve has now reached a length of 11 in (28 cm). There are 40/44/48/52/58/62/66 sts on the needles.

Continue to work in stockinette stitch in the round until the Sleeve measures 15/15.25/15.75/16.25/16.5/17/17.25 in (38/39/40/41/42/43/44 cm) from the underarm. At this point, the Sleeve can be lengthened or shortened according to your personal preferences. Change to US 6 (4.0 mm) needles and work 2.25 in (6 cm) in 1 × 1 ribbing. Bind off all stitches.

Work the 2nd Sleeve the same way.

Finishing

Place the 7 previously held stitches on the inside of the right half of the Collar (as viewed while the garment is worn) onto US 8 (5.0 mm) needles. Join new working yarn, and work the following 2 rows 22 times:

Row 1 (RS): Selv st, k5, selv st.
Row 2 (WS): Selv st, p5, selv st.

Transfer these 7 sts to a stitch holder or safety pin for holding. Then place the 7 previously held stitches on the inside of the left half of the Collar onto US 8 (5.0 mm) needles. Join new working yarn, and here, too, work the following 2 rows 22 times:

Row 1 (RS): Selv st, k5, selv st.
Row 2 (WS): Selv st, p5, selv st.

In the next RS row, join the left and right facing strip as follows: Selv st, k6, cast on 1 new stitch. Take up the previously held stitches of the 2nd facing strip again and k6, selv st.

Work another 1.25 in (3 cm) in stockinette stitch in turned rows, then bind off all stitches.

Open the zipper, pin it between Front and facing strip using tailor pins, then sew it in using sewing thread and short, neat stitches.

Attach both facing strips to the Front using sewing thread and short, neat stitches, creating a clean finish. Weave in all ends and wash the sweater in lukewarm water with a mild wool detergent. Block it spread out flat on an even, horizontal surface, and let it dry.

KNITTING CHARTS

Sizes 1/2/3/4, Left Front

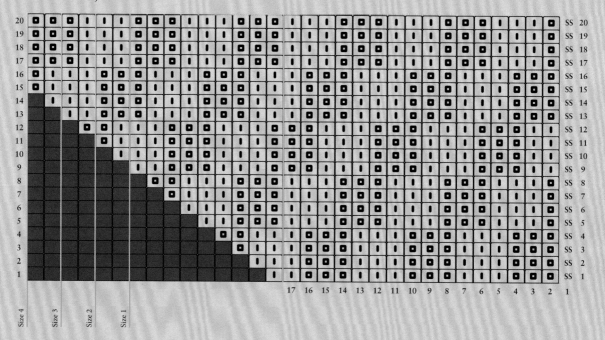

Sizes 1/2/3/4, Back

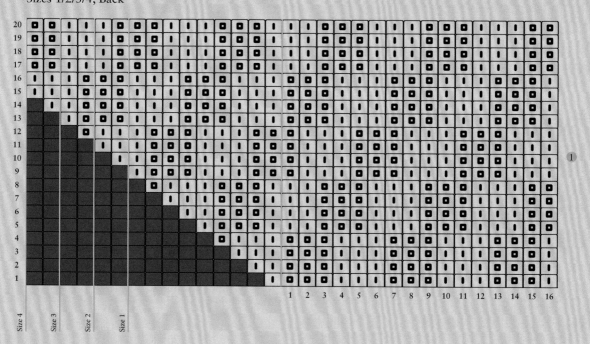

Sizes 1/2/3/4, Right Front

Knitting Symbols

▣	= knit	SS = selvedge stitch(es)
▮	= purl	■ = no stitch, for a better overview only

Sizes 5/6/7, Left Front

Sizes 5/6/7, Back

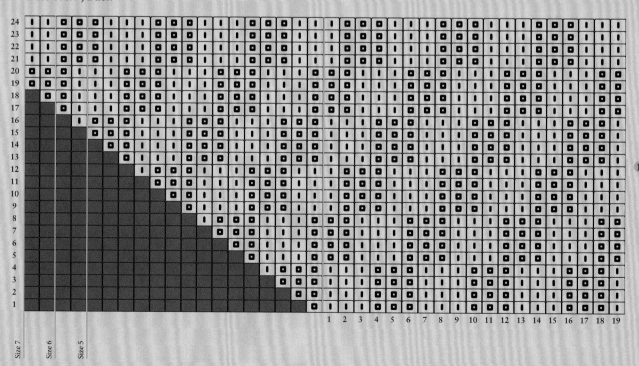

Sizes 5/6/7, Right Front

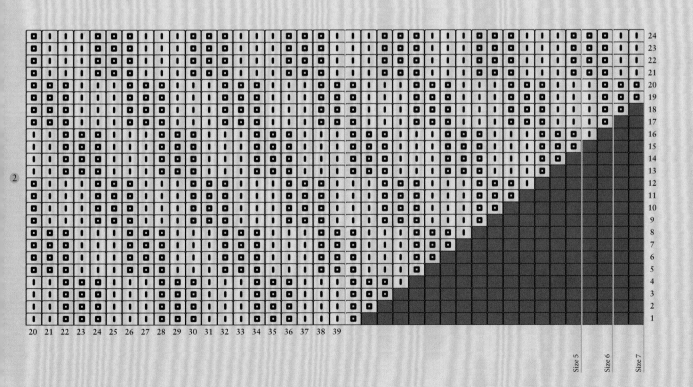

About the Author

Clarissa's first knitting project was a sweater for her favorite teddy about 30 years ago, and she has been knitting ever since.

After a successful career in knitwear design and creative buying at various fashion brands, the fashion design major returned to hand knitting in 2019, when maternity leave with her young daughter suddenly decelerated her life and afforded her plenty of room for creativity.

Since 2020, Clarissa has been designing hand-knitting patterns under her label "Cozyknits." Her style is timeless yet modern, and she is especially fond of distinctive details and contemporary lines.

Clarissa's creative mind is buzzing with countless designs, every detail thought out from the first stitch to the last—just waiting to take shape in the most beautiful yarns. Knitting is her passion, and she finds having the opportunity to be creative fulfilling—it makes her very happy day after day.

Find Clarissa on Instagram @clarissaschellong

On her website: www.cozyknits.de

Show your own projects using hashtag #cozyknits
We are looking forward to seeing your masterpieces!

www.cozyknits.de

www.ravelry.com/designers/clarissa-schellong

Thank You

It is not the happy ones who are grateful—it is the grateful ones who are happy.

At this point, I would like to express my thanks to all who have supported me in making the dream of bringing this book to life come true for me.

From the bottom of my heart, thank you to Melanie Kowalski, my mentor from the editing department of EMF Publishing's craft division, for the great idea and concept. The professional collaboration with you was a great pleasure from the first day on!

A big thank you also goes to Annerose Sieck, my editor and the good angel in the background of this book. I would also like to thank the yarn manufacturers who so generously supported this project with the absolutely most beautiful yarns. A heartfelt thank you to the Lamana, Pascuali, Lang Yarns, and Rauwerk companies for believing in me and trusting me to come up with designs to suit the essence of their yarns!

From the bottom of my heart, thank you, Nadine, for giving me the nudge I needed to write these patterns. You are a treasure and were always right: I had nothing to lose, but so much to gain.

And now I will move on to my sample knitters Mirjam Riedmann, Miriam Führer, Stefanie Kaiser, Susanne Hagemann, and last but not least Nicole Anthimosoglou: Girls, with all due respect, without you, there would have been no book! It is such an honor to know that I have people by my side who completely, selflessly support me and my dream with so much time, energy, effort, and love and who have spent weeks making sure that all the ideas in my mind were turned into beautiful samples. Thank you from the bottom of my heart! What a lucky girl I am to have you all!

And to my mom: Thank you! Not only did you knit like a fiend and far out of your comfort zone, you taught me to knit in the first place and, without you, there would be no book. Thank you from the bottom of my heart for your tireless support, not only in knitting but in all aspects of life and whenever I need you. I get to go through life with the feeling that basically nothing can happen to me because I have parents who catch me when I fall. I'm sure that's why it's so easy for me to smile on so many days. Mom, Dad, thank you for always being there for me. I am so happy to have you!

I've saved the most important for last: My family. Alex, thank you! Thank you for putting up with all my insecurities and moods. Thank you for bearing with me for so long because that's indeed not always easy. When we got married, I mentioned that I get through so much in life because you believe in me so much—you hold fresh proof of that in your hands now. Thank you for all the days you freed me from menial tasks. Thank you for never questioning me. Thank you for being proud of me.

And just as important: Thank you to you, my favorite little human! You bring me the greatest happiness! You are the sunshine of my life.

STACKPOLE BOOKS

An imprint of The Globe Pequot Publishing Group, Inc.
64 South Main Street
Essex, CT 06426
www.globepequot.com

Distributed by NATIONAL BOOK NETWORK
800-462-6420

© Edition Michael Fischer GmbH, 2022
www.emf-verlag.de
This edition of UNISEX-PULLOVER STRICKEN first published in Germany by Edition Michael Fischer GmbH in 2022 is published by arrangement with Silke Bruenink Agency, Munich, Germany.

Book layout: Luca Feigs
Product management: Melanie Kowalski
Typesetting: Eva Krebs, Luca Feigs
Photographs: © Corinna Teresa Brix, Munich, Germany; Step-by-step photos and photos in chapter Basics: © Clarissa Schellong
Illustrations in chapter Basics: Ina Langguth, Berlin, Germany
Editing: Annerose Sieck, Neumünster, Germany
Translation: Katharina Sokiran

British Library Cataloguing in Publication Information available

Library of Congress Cataloging-in-Publication Data available

ISBN 978-0-8117-7491-8 (paper : alk. paper)
ISBN 978-0-8117-7492-5 (electronic)